BLOOD, TOIL, TEARS AND SWEAT

BOOKS BY JOHN LUKACS

The Great Powers and Eastern Europe

*Tocqueville: The European Revolution and Correspondence
    with Gobineau (editor)*

A History of the Cold War

Decline and Rise of Europe

A New History of the Cold War

Historical Consciousness

The Passing of the Modern Age

A Sketch of the History of Chestnut Hill College, 1924–1974

The Last European War, 1939–1941

1945: Year Zero

Philadelphia: Patricians and Philistines, 1900–1950

*Outgrowing Democracy: A History of the United States in the
    Twentieth Century*

Budapest 1900: A Historical Portrait of a City and Its Culture

Confessions of an Original Sinner

*The Duel: 10 May–31 July; The Eighty-Day Struggle Between
    Churchill and Hitler*

BLOOD, TOIL, TEARS AND SWEAT

The Dire Warning

JOHN LUKACS

BASIC
BOOKS

A Member of the Perseus Books Group
New York

Books published by Basic Books are available at special discounts for bulk
purchases in the United States by corporations, institutions, and other
organizations. For more information, please contact the Special Markets
Department at the Perseus Books Group, 2300 Chestnut Street, Suite 200,
Philadelphia, PA 19103, or call (800) 810-4145, ext. 5000, or e-mail
special.markets@perseusbooks.com.

Design by Jane Raese
Text set in Bulmer

Cataloging-in-Publication Data for this book is available from
the Library of Congress.
ISBN 978-046-500287-0

10 9 8 7 6 5 4 3 2 1

TO MICHAEL

Hic parvum opus dedican

Contents

BLOOD, TOIL, TEARS AND SWEAT

Behind the Horseman Sat Black Care

Post equitem sedet atra cura

—*Ode,* HORACE 3.1.41

CHAPTER ONE

I have nothing to offer but

blood, toil, tears, and sweat.

PHRASES ARE REMEMBERED, recalled often, for many different reasons. Their endurance and the respect paid to them after many years are the only marks of their value. This is so for any work of art, whether a painting or a piece of music, no matter how it was thought of at the time of its appearance. A bad poem will not much survive, a good poem will. But now consider another question: What did it mean at the very time of its appearance? Has it changed since then? In 1940 some of Winston Churchill's speeches altered the course of British, of European, of world history. But "blood, toil, tears, and sweat" did not—at least not on or about 13th of May 1940, when he spoke those words.

So why direct our attention to these words? Because they sound impressive in retrospect? Yes, but there is more than that. They cast a sudden stab of light beneath—beneath, not beyond—the sonorous timbre of Churchill's rhetoric. They illuminate something. They reflect something that was and remains beneath their bravery. Churchill's bravery was extant in May 1940; people, especially in Britain, were impressed with it; others would acknowledge it but qualify it in other terms: bravery, if you so wish, but the bravery of a man intoxicated with his ambitions, unsteady, voluble, imprudent, trumpeting with *braggadocio*, an un-English word, or "pride before the fall," a very English phrase. In time many of the men and women who disliked him were to be proved wrong. But not yet.

What they did not know—and what not many people, including even some historians, do not know now, nearly seventy years later—was that beneath Churchill's bravery lay his understanding of a looming catastrophe, still unimaginable to most: that it was late, probably too late, that Adolf Hitler was winning, that he was about to win, that he was close to winning the Second World War, his war.

MAY 1940—IT EVOKES LITTLE or nothing in the minds
of most Americans. But in the minds of Western Europeans whose countries were invaded and overrun by
Hitler's German armies during that month, it evokes large
and dark and sometimes uneasily suppressed memories.
As for the British, their memory of May 1940 is simpler.
The news from across the Channel was bad. But Churchill
had become their prime minister, they were inspired by
his resolution, he and they were now bound together, he
and they trusted that Britain would endure and win the
war in the end. During and well after the war that was what
Churchill wanted them, and the English-speaking peoples
of the world, to remember: that was what and how he
wrote about May 1940 in his own inimitable history of the
Second World War. True enough but not *quite* true in May
1940—surely not on the 13th of that month. And Churchill knew *that* too.

He knew that Adolf Hitler was winning the war. *His*
war, which was nothing less than the Second World War.
Nearly a century after the outbreak of the First World War,
historians and others are still mulling over and debating

who were most responsible for what happened in 1914: Austria, Serbia, Germany, Russia, France, Britain; monarchs, prime ministers, ambassadors, general staffs, etc., etc. All of them were responsible to some degree or other. About 1939 there can be (or, rather, ought to be) no such question. One man, Hitler, started that war. The responsibilities of other people and other governments in 1939 were, at worst, those of omission, not of commission.

Yet Hitler was not happy when, two days after his army crashed into Poland, the British (and French) governments, even though reluctantly, declared war against his German Reich. He hoped that in the last minute they would relent—as they had relented a year before, at Munich—especially now, when Stalin's Soviet Union had moved to his side and made a pact with him. Yet the British and the French declarations of war came nevertheless—even though, as soon appeared, they were unready to fight with full force. But the main reason why he chose to invade Poland and risk a war with Britain and France in September 1939 was not the obsession of a fanatic. He thought that time was working against him and his Germany. He had to fulfill his mission—the German domination of Eastern Europe and his consequent primacy over most of Europe—before the Western democracies armed themselves and became stronger. His friend and ally Mussolini suggested to him that this was not so: The French and the British were not ready for such an effort. But for Hitler, if war had to come, better now rather than later.* And he was not altogether wrong: In 1940 the French collapsed and Britain was still largely unarmed.

There was another element in Hitler's mind about the war. This was a matter not of timing but of ideas. He believed that Germany was now largely his (which was not really untrue) and that the German people now had a quality that was so much better than were the qualities of his enemies. This was not a quality of their race or their physical composition. It was mental, not material; spiritual, not biological. It was a result of their adoption of and acceptance of National Socialism. Shortly before May 1940, in talking with Goebbels, Hitler said that this war was but a repetition, on a larger scale, of what had been happening in Germany before his coming to power. In the brutal street fighting two or three years before 1933, one National Socialist storm trooper was worth two or three of his

---

*There was another, personal element. At some time—mostly in 1938—he convinced himself, probably wrongly, that he would not have many more years to live. Hence he had to complete his task. There are many scattered evidences of this odd pessimistic hypochondria, one of his few weaknesses.

opponents, say, two Englishmen or three Frenchmen. Not
because of the better equipment and better training of
German soldiers but because of the superior determina-
tion, courage, and spirit of his soldiers: because the Wehr-
macht, the Kriegsmarine, the Luftwaffe, no matter their
differences and commanders, were a new model German
armed force. He was convinced of the inherent truth of
this. He thought that the relations and the contests of
states, armies, and nations were like those of individuals.*
Before 1933 he was certain that he would, almost inevitably, arrive to power in Germany. Before 1940 he believed that his Germany may dominate Europe. In May
1940 he had reason to believe that.

He was not alone in thinking this. Hitler's Germans,
wrote Robert Boothby, a Churchillian, a few months before, "represented the incredible conception of a *movement*—young, virile, dynamic, and violent—which is
advancing irresistibly to overthrow a decaying old world,

---

*Was he entirely wrong? Proust, in a fragment, 1915: "The life
of nations merely repeats, on a larger scale, the lives of their
component cells; and he who is incapable of understanding the
mystery, the reactions, the laws that determine the movements
of the individual, can never hope to say anything worth while
listening to about the struggles of nations."

that we must continually bear in mind, for it is the main source of the Nazi strength and power." *Germany Turns the Clock Back* was the title of a best-selling and well-written book about Hitler and Germany by Edgar Mowrer, an intelligent American journalist. But the opposite was true. Hitler had moved the clock *forward*. Germany was modern; her industry, her army, her air force were more modern than those of their opponents; the Third Reich was more modern than Poland, Denmark, Norway, Holland, Belgium, France, Britain—its victims and adversaries. So was the ideology of National Socialism more modern than Liberalism, parliamentarism, Marxism; the new Reich more modern than the ramshackle republics and the remnant constitutional monarchies of Europe. National Socialist Germany was—it surely seemed—an incarnation of a wave, perhaps *the* wave, of the future. Millions of people in Europe thought that, or at least something like that; and in May and June in 1940 many more millions came to think that too.

Some of this was opportunism, an amazed reaction to the stunning successes of the German army, but there was more to it too. Evidences of this, including the inclinations and expressions of many thinkers and writers and artists in many countries of Europe, would fill a one-thousand page book. These were accumulating all through May, June, and July 1940. After all, before 1940 there were three great prototypes of political standards and states: parliamentary democracy incarnated by the English-speaking nations and most states of Western Europe; Communism, represented by the Soviet Union; and nationalist dictatorships, of which the prime incarnation was National Socialist Germany. In 1940, as also for some years before and then for some years thereafter, National Socialist Germany was the strongest of the three. We know—and often forget—that eventually it took the combined forces of the United States, Soviet Russia, and Great Britain to defeat and conquer it, and that the alliance of any two of them was not sufficient for that.

But the subject of *this* book is one particular sentence said by one particular man on the 13th of May 1940, a man who—perhaps uniquely, and providentially—understood Hitler.*

---

*It is noteworthy that they had never met. In 1932 Hitler, who at that time was eager and willing to meet all kinds of Englishmen, oddly refused to meet Churchill. In 1937 it was Churchill who thought it best not to visit Germany and meet Hitler.

THE 13TH OF MAY 1940 was Whitmonday, customarily a holiday in much of Europe before the war. What we know about Hitler is that on that day he was confident but also nervous. Three days before, at dawn on the 10th, a Friday, he had launched the great Western offensive of his armies against Holland, Belgium, Luxembourg, and France. On the 13th, he was in his headquarters behind the front: Putting his recently prescribed glasses on and off, he peered hour after hour over the maps, satisfied with the rate of the advance of his troops but not quite sure of what was to come, and how soon. He, whose entire strategy was a kind of reversal of Clausewitz—for Hitler politics was a continuation of war by other means—paid little attention to politics that day, including political intelligence from the camps of his adversaries. Three days before, late in the evening of his longest day, the tenth, the news had come that Winston Churchill had become the prime minister of Great Britain. That night he had paid no attention to that.*

---

*Goebbels wrote in his diary late on 10 May: "Churchill is now Premier. The field is clear! That's what we like." Now note what Goebbels wrote in the same diary on 18 June 1941 (three days before the German invasion of Russia) about Churchill: "Were it not for him, this war would have ended long ago."

CHURCHILL HAD—for an Englishman—an exceptional knowledge and comprehension of Europe, of the history and of the character of many of its nations. He was a convinced and committed Francophile, for more than political reasons—an inclination that emerged well before the French-British entente and alliance before and during the First World War. More important, for our purposes, is his view of Germany and of the Germans. He was both impressed and at least somewhat repelled by the military rigidity of Prussianism, as early as his visit to Germany in 1909. His reaction was not unusual. Prusso- and Germanophobia prevailed among Englishmen and Americans throughout the First World War, sometimes unduly so. Too often they attributed the elements of Prussianism to Germany as a whole.

More unusual and enduring was Churchill's respect—respect rather than admiration, but true respect nonetheless—for what Germany and the Germans were able to achieve during the First World War. He thought, and feared, that their defeat in 1918 might not be the end of it. It is telling what he wrote in the 1920s, at the very end of his massive history of the First World War, *The World Crisis*:

> The German people are worthy of better explanations than the shallow tale that they were undermined by enemy propaganda. . . .
>
> For four years Germany fought and defied the five continents of the world by land and sea and air. The German armies upheld their tottering confederates, intervened in every theatre with success, stood everywhere on conquered territory, and inflicted on their enemies more than twice the bloodshed they suffered themselves. To break their strength and science and curb their fury, it was necessary to bring all the greatest nations of mankind into the field against them. Overwhelming populations, unlimited resources, measureless sacrifice, the Sea Blockade, could not prevail for fifty months. Small states were trampled down in the struggle; a mighty Empire was battered into unrecognizable fragments; and nearly twenty million men perished or shed their blood before the sword was wrested from that terrible hand. Surely, Germans, for history it is enough!
>
> [And] . . . Is this the end? Is it to be merely a chapter in a cruel and senseless story? Will a new

generation in their turn be immolated to square the black accounts of Teuton and Gaul? Will our children bleed and gasp again in devastated lands? Or will there spring from the very fires of conflict that reconciliation of the three giant combatants, which would unite their genius and secure to each in safety and freedom a share in rebuilding the glory of Europe?

In October 1930 a small episode occurred in Churchill's life that he himself did not record nor even perhaps recall.* Churchill and his wife were dining at the German Embassy in London. He kept asking his hosts about Hitler. One of the hosts, an official of the embassy and a descendant of Bismarck, found this so strange that he reported it, in a routine dispatch, to Berlin. "Hitler of course declared he does not intend starting a world war but Churchill believes that Hitler and his followers will grasp the first chance to resort to arms again . . ." One month before that dinner, Hitler and his National Socialist Party had made an impressive gain in the German national elec-

---

*It may be found in the mountains of German diplomatic documents between the wars, and even printed among the thousands of documents selected for inclusion in one of their volumes.

tions. But no one at that time thought that a man such as Hitler could ever become the elected leader or chancellor of Germany.

Hitler did. He became chancellor in January 1933—at a time when Churchill's career, his influence, and his political prospects were at their lowest. Over the course of the 1930s, Churchill's career went from failure to failure as Hitler added success to success. The two were not unrelated. Churchill's reputation in the 1930s suffered because of, among other things, his insistence on the German danger.

Alone in the House of Commons, Churchill spoke year after year, often month after month, about what he saw as the most ominous of perils: Germany was arming while Britain was not; Germany was getting ready for war, Britain was not. Alone, because *very* few people listened to him for many years. Labour was still wed to pacifism and disarmament; many of its members regarded Churchill as an imperialist, their inveterate adversary, for many years. What was worse: Save for a handful of men, most of them his friends, Churchill's main enemies were the Conservatives—the majority party, his party.

The Conservatives distrusted Churchill, that maverick, for many reasons. In the 1930s, for the first time, Germany was one of those reasons. Slowly, gradually, the British hatred for the Germany of the First World War was dissolving, at the very time when Hitler came to power in Berlin. Throughout the British upper and middle classes there was a vague general feeling that the terms imposed on the Germans in the Versailles Treaty were unduly severe and injurious. There was an even stronger and more widespread sense that another war must not ever come; that Britain and the Empire must never again be involved in an armed struggle in Europe. There was yet another, newer, element as well: a fear of Communism, a disdain and dislike of Soviet Russia. That state, not Germany, was the enemy of civilisation. Hitler's National Socialism (like Mussolini's Fascism) was not something for Britain, but it was much less dangerous than and much preferable to Communism and Soviet Russia. Therefore, Germany should be given at least some benefit of the doubt.

That was the essence of the word "appeasement"—even now debated—a word that held no negative connotations before 1939. If, to avoid trouble and, God save us, war, Germany must be appeased, so be it: In any event, that was worth more than a try, or even more than one try. That was, by and large, the belief (and the ideology) of the great majority of Conservatives and especially their members in Parliament; they were the kind of men whom the British people elected with a large majority in 1935. They disdained Churchill and paid no attention to his sputtering warnings: he was wrong—and so often—in the past, so he was also surely wrong now. The harsh brutalities of the Hitler regime, especially its treatment of Jews, made little impression on these Conservatives; these matters were regrettable, at worst.

By 1937 the chasm between the rank-and-file Conservatives and Churchill had grown. Even more than his bumbling and provincially British predecessor Stanley Baldwin, the new prime minister Neville Chamberlain, shared just about all of these latent (and sometimes open) prejudices in favor of Germany and of what he considered the governing necessity of appeasing Hitler when and if possible. Thus in 1938, when Hitler's march across Central Europe began, the year turned out to be the most triumphant of his entire career and coincided with the worst year of Churchill's career, worse even than the fall of his power and reputation in 1915, after the failure of the Dardanelles.* After the Munich settlement in late September 1938, when Chamberlain gave in to Hitler, Churchill

---

*One reason for his unpopularity was his impetuous (and, in retrospect, unnecessary) championing of Edward VIII and his American mistress, Mrs. Simpson, in the monarchical and constitutional crisis in December 1936.

made a sonorous, impressive, and well-nigh prophetic speech in Parliament; he was nearly disavowed by the Conservative men and women of Epping, his own constituency.*

Five months later there came a change. Hitler broke his agreement at Munich, and Chamberlain was forced to make plans to resist him; another five months later war came, and Churchill was brought into the British government; and another eight months later he became prime minister and the leader of Great Britain. But the title of one of the best of the hundreds of books written about Churchill, *Churchill: A Study of Failure* by the excellent Robert Rhodes James, is accurate. Churchill's career was marked

---

*In two matters Churchill was wrong about Munich. He thought and said that Britain and France should have gone to war with Germany because of Czechoslovakia. But Britain and France were not ready in 1938; they (and their public) were readier in 1939. (Hitler knew that: He said later that he regretted the Munich "settlement," that he would have preferred to risk war in 1938.) The other matter was Churchill's belief (which he, by and large, repeated in his war memoirs ten years later, after the war) that Soviet Russia was ready to join the war against Germany in 1938 (when Moscow had an alliance signed with France and Czechoslovakia) but then not in 1939. This was not so. Stalin was ready to get off the hook in 1938.

by many failures—until September 1939 and in many ways even after that. And when he became prime minister, were his, and Britain's, prospects better? Not at all.

MUCH OF WHAT HAPPENED in May 1940 involves the relationship of Chamberlain and Churchill.

Their views of Germany and Hitler had differed enough to render them adversaries. But in March 1939 Chamberlain was forced to revise his views—at least somewhat. Hitler had broken his word he had given at Munich; on 15 March the German army marched into Prague and annexed what had remained of Czechoslovakia to the German Reich. What followed was a revolution of British opinion: this far, many people thought and said, but no farther. Chamberlain, not without reluctance, relented. He and his government now thought—reasonably—that the only way to stop Hitler from advancing farther was to let him know that Britain would oppose that, if necessary, by war. (They wished to avoid the fatal German misunderstanding a quarter of a century before, in 1914, when the German regime was not certain whether Britain would go to war to defend France and Belgium.) So the British government gave a guarantee to Poland, the next evident object of German aggression.

Chamberlain was still inclined not to accept the eventual inevitability of war. But by the end of August he did not have much of a choice. Reluctantly the British government declared war on Germany two days after the German armies crashed into Poland.

By that time Churchill was part of Chamberlain's government. Throughout the preceding months Churchill's reputation had begun to rise. He was, after all, right rather than wrong about Hitler, people said. On 1 September 1939 Chamberlain offered him the post of First Lord of the Admiralty, chief of the British Navy, the post that Churchill had twenty-five years before. There followed the eight months of hesitant British-French warfare against Germany, the so-called "phony war." Phony except at sea: On the oceans of the globe there were a few limited naval victories (but also a few defeats) for England.

Then came a dramatic change of the war in Scandinavia. On 9 April 1940, Hitler's army and navy invaded Denmark and Norway. The British response, including even the performance of her navy, was by and large dilatory, stumbling, inefficient. Churchill was largely responsible for that. But while Chamberlain's popularity fell, Churchill's went on to rise—until, on 10 May, Chamberlain gave up his command. Churchill eagerly grasped the wheel of the ship of state.

Such is the irony of history (or the tides of national sentiment). How this came about, in the first ten days of May 1940, has been recounted often. It was, in its way, a shining episode in the history of parliamentary democracy: the capability of the elected representatives of a people to change their leaders at a critical moment. But that transition was not simple; and the sentiments and the inclinations of those who had to abandon Chamberlain were not simple at all. By the beginning of May the British people knew that their armed forces in and around Norway had failed. They were, at long last, impatient with the direction of the war. Chamberlain was a good man, they sensed, but not a war leader; he did not have his heart in that. Churchill, in contrast, was a warrior. The so-called Norway Debate in the House of Commons began on 7 May and went on for two days. A small group of Churchillians were vocal, some of them declaring that Chamberlain had to go. They were supported by the minority, by Labour and by the Liberals. What was more important, indeed decisive, was that some of the Chamberlainite Conservatives were also relinquishing their leader. When the vote came on 8 May, the government majority fell by one hundred.

Chamberlain was no longer obstinate. He said that

perhaps he ought to resign. On 9 May Chamberlain asked Churchill to come to his office. They agreed that there must be a national government, including Labour. Churchill knew that his hour had come. But that was not yet definite. Halifax, the foreign secretary, with a temperament and a view of the world quite different from Churchill's, was also a possible successor. Halifax did not much trust Churchill. But he did not much wish to be prime minister, either. As a peer, he thought, he would not have enough power in the House of Commons to wage a war. That was a constitutional glitch that could be overcome. More important was Halifax's unspoken belief (and that of many other Conservatives) that, with the state of public opinion as it was, Churchill must be given the post—even though he might not last long.

Then, on the morning of Friday the 10th came the thunderous news: Hitler's armies had burst forth in the west. The German invasion of Holland, Belgium, Luxembourg, and, behind them, France, had begun. The news reached Chamberlain and Churchill at dawn. Churchill got up at 7, early for him. He consumed his considerable breakfast and left Admiralty House for an early meeting of the War Cabinet. There he found that Chamberlain may have been changing his mind: He said that perhaps he should stay on until the coming great battle in Belgium would be decided. But now Chamberlain no longer had support from many of his former friends. Everyone agreed that a national government must be formed.

Churchill, contrary to his habits, did not speak much. It was not until 5 in the afternoon that the Labour politicians, amidst their annual conference in Bornemouth, telephoned to say that they would not join a government led by Chamberlain but would do so under Churchill. A few minutes before 6 Chamberlain left for Buckingham Palace to hand the seals of his office to the King. George VI was not happy. He liked Chamberlain; even more, he liked Halifax. He had hoped for the latter, but that was not to be.

Half an hour later Churchill's driver took him to the palace. They had a very English conversation. The King, to make things easier, said with a faint gesture of humor: "I suppose you don't know why I have sent for you?" Churchill replied: "Sir, I simply couldn't imagine why." The King replied: "I want you to form a Government."

IT WAS ABOUT 7 O'CLOCK, the end of a beautiful day, London placid in a blue twilight. There was nothing yet in the newspapers about the new government. Back at

Admiralty House, Churchill immediately sat down to work, writing and dictating letters, way into the night. One of the first letters he wrote was to Chamberlain. Among other matters he said that there was no need for the Chamberlains to move from Downing Street; he, Churchill, would stay in Admiralty House, at least for another month.

The gesture had an effect on Chamberlain. He and his wife liked to live in Downing Street. (In 1937 Mrs. Chamberlain had made significant changes in the domestic architecture of Ten Downing Street.) They were grateful to Churchill for this generous gesture. But that was more than a gesture: It was typical of Churchill, whose prime virtue was magnanimity, something even larger and deeper than generosity. There are evidences of it throughout his long life. One of the effects of his magnanimity was his inclination to forgive and to forget unpleasant things. Chamberlain's mind and his temperament were narrower than Churchill's, but the latter's magnanimity made a great impression on him; it was the realization of something to which he was entirely and temperamentally unaccustomed. Eight months before, Chamberlain was compelled—uneasily—to include Churchill in his government. They had been, after all, public opponents, even enemies, for two if not more years before; he knew some of the sharp, cutting things that Churchill had said about him; in turn, he had tried everything to thwart and reduce Churchill, including, on occasion, having the latter's private telephone tapped. Yet from the moment Churchill was admitted to his government, his loyalty to Chamberlain was more than unexceptionable: It was absolute. Not one public or private remark was uttered by Churchill even during the gloomiest and most unpromising months of the phony war. More important, and more recently, during the three days of debate in the House of Commons, Churchill stood up saying that he took full responsibility for the errors and shortcomings made in Norway; he spoke not a single word suggestive as criticism of Chamberlain. Something more than political calculation was in Churchill's behavior, and Chamberlain sensed that.

All of this had lasting and beneficial consequences now that Churchill had become prime minister. Chamberlain had become grateful to and appreciative of Churchill. Churchill continued to treat him with much more than expectable respect. The result was that at the end of May, when facing the greatest possible catastrophe—the British army encircled at Dunkirk—Halifax contradicted Churchill, saying in the secret cabinet (and not without reason) that the government should at least attempt to ascertain what Hitler might propose; Chamberlain did not quite side with Halifax. Had he done so, Churchill's position might have become untenable. Once Chamberlain's support of Halifax would have become known, there would have been a movement within the Conservative Party to disembarrass themselves of Churchill. But that did not happen. What did happen was an example of something that is, alas, all too rare in human affairs: magnanimity bearing providential results.

THE 10TH OF MAY—a day of providential coincidence: Hitler's momentous lunge forward that morning; Churchill's momentous nomination to the prime ministership that night. Churchill was not a religious person. Yet he believed that what had come to him that day was due to Providence of which he was but an instrument. He remembered and wrote about that day many years later in his war memoirs, in his *History of the Second World War*. "As I went to bed about 3 A.M., I was conscious of a profound sense of relief. At last I had the authority to give directions over the whole scene. I felt as if I were walking with Destiny, and that all my past life had been but a preparation for this hour and for this trial."

We need not doubt his words. But there is a duality in every human being. Note his last two words: "this trial." For trial the war would become—and trial already it was, something that he perhaps knew better than anyone else. He knew what kind of enormous might and strength his country had to face. The day may have been bright, but the prospects were dark. There is one telling evidence that Churchill knew that already: Late that afternoon, as he left the King and was driven back to Admiralty House, he was silent. Next to him, behind the driver, sat Inspector W. H. Thompson, his old bodyguard. In the last minute before pulling up to Admiralty House, Churchill spoke. He said that Thompson surely knew why he had been called by the King. Thompson said, yes; he congratulated Churchill and added, "I only wish the position had come your way in better times, for you have an enormous task."

Churchill's eyes suddenly filled with tears. "God alone knows how great it is," he said to Thompson. "I hope it is not too late. I am very much afraid it is." He added, "We can only do our best."

Behind the horseman sat black care.

Churchill bit his lip and lifted himself out of the car.

CHAPTER TWO

Easter came very early in 1940, and so did Whitsun. In Britain the government cancelled the Whitmonday holiday. The 10th of May was a Friday. The momentous news of the war notwithstanding, a kind of weekend calm prevailed in London. The weather was sunlit and brilliant, and remained so throughout almost all of May. People thought, reasonably and almost without exception, that the great battle for Western Europe had just begun, that it was too early to tell what was going to happen. The news they had from the newspapers and the radio was fragmentary, inaccurate, and generally confident. But across the Channel, by Monday the 13th —the fourth day into their Western European campaign—Hitler's armies were winning their war, *the* war.

Some of that was the result of their superior planning. The Franco-British plan was to move north into Belgium and Holland the day they were invaded, and then confront the German armies on a line running for the most part along the rivers of Belgium and southern Holland. The German plan, drafted by General Manstein *and* by Hitler himself, was to strike straight to the west, cutting off those Allied armies to the north, making for the Channel coast and ports as soon as possible. The plan's code-name was "Sichelschnitt," a sickle-cut, a horizontal slash (unlike their famous Schlieffen Plan of 1914, which was a largely vertical move like the cut of a scythe, advancing southward along an arc).

The excellence of Sichelschnitt's execution matched the excellence of the plan. In Holland the canals and waters and what there was of a Dutch army nowhere halted the German advance. In Belgium the resistance of the national army was sporadic and feeble. What was more important: The French (and indirectly the British) war planners thought that in southeastern Belgium the Ardennes mountains were largely unsuitable for mobile warfare and that the Germans would avoid them. To the contrary: They moved across the Ardennes with ease. Their tanks and other armored motors ground ahead in what was then a still new method of warfare. In 1914 the German forward troops had picked up the frontier barriers and then tried to push the entire line of frontier forward. In 1940 they were like armored spears, ferrous tips of armies thrown ahead. By Sunday night their spearheads had cut across southeastern Belgium and were entering France. By Monday they were at the widest river yet to be traversed, the Meuse. That afternoon—about the very hour when Churchill entered the House of Commons and began to speak—they began crossing the Meuse at points not far from a French town with a name reverberating from an ominous past: Sedan. They were led by a general whose name would be reverberating in the future: Rommel.

The extent of this German advance was not yet known anywhere in the world. Even the French general staff did not recognize what a catastrophe had come until the next day. But somehow the sense that Hitler was winning was palpable throughout Europe. Late in the afternoon of Monday the 13th, Mussolini told his son-in-law and foreign minister, Ciano: "Today I tell you that [the Allies] have lost the war. Any delay is inconceivable. We have no time to lose. Within a month I shall declare war." Later that night Hitler dictated a letter to Mussolini: Germany is victorious on land and, above all, in the air.

BEHIND THE HORSEMAN SAT BLACK CARE.

Churchill, better than many others, understood the power of Britain's enemies. But in connection with that, there was his other concern: not about foreign enemies but about his domestic opponents—those within his own party, the majority in Parliament. "Mr. Chamberlain was their chosen leader," he wrote after the war. "I could not but realize that his supersession by me must be very unpleasant to many of them, after all my long years of criticism and often fierce reproach." He listed or, rather, summarized his many conflicts with them. "To accept me as Prime Minister was to them very difficult. It caused pain to many honourable men." So it was. Then he added two sentences, concluding his paragraph: "None of these considerations caused me the slightest anxiety. I knew they were all drowned by the cannonade."

Well, not quite so. Or, at best, not yet. We may be able to reconstruct much of this from the kind of evidence that now, almost seventy years later, has become regrettably rare: records of words written. In 1940, many members of the upper and middle classes of Britain still kept diaries and wrote letters. Such written evidences are not only more concrete than memories of spoken words but the very quality of their authenticity is stronger. Writing, after all, is the result of a definite impulse of self-expression: As T. S. Eliot once put it, it is "the desire to vanquish a mental preoccupation by expressing it consciously and clearly." Of course much depends on who the writer is. On 9 May, "Chips" Channon—an interminable diary-writer, American-born, for many years a Conservative M.P., a champion snob, very rich, a know-it-all, and an unconditional admirer and follower of Chamberlain—wrote in his diary: "Perhaps the darkest day in English history. I sat numb with misery, and mused on this fantastic day." The next day, Lord Hankey—a more stolid and respectable public official—wrote in a letter to his son: "The net result of it all is that today, when the greatest battle of our history has begun, when the fate of the whole Empire is at stake, we are to have a government of politicians . . . quite a number of whom are perfectly futile people." On the same day, Joseph Kennedy, the American ambassador—Chamberlain's friend and Churchill's foe—

telegraphed to Washington that Chamberlain, Halifax, and Churchill were tired old men.*

Early on saturday, 11 May, Churchill set himself to the task of composing his government. Early that morning he asked Chamberlain and Halifax to come over to Admiralty House to look at the war situation. Churchill told them that "the Belgians are reported to be fighting well. The Dutch are also making a stubborn resistance." This was not so; but there was, as yet, no evidence before him to question that. Churchill nonetheless knew what he and the British people were up against. Around noon he was driven to Ten Downing Street, before which there had gathered a small crowd of common people. Some of them cried out: "Good luck, Winnie. God bless you." Churchill turned to Lord Ismay. Again he had tears in his eyes:

---

*To Chamberlain Kennedy said that he couldn't see how Britain could carry on if the French gave up. Chamberlain wrote in a letter to his sister: "I did not see how we could either." (One of Churchill's liabilities with the Conservatives was what they saw as his excessive trust of the French.)

"Poor people. I can give them nothing but disaster for quite a long time"—words in accord with those he would intone in Parliament two days later.

He said to Chamberlain: "I am in your hands." One outcome of this was that Churchill did not much change the Cabinet—though he was bringing some of his supporters into government posts.*

Halifax, the foreign secretary, was more critical than was Chamberlain (now with the title Lord President of the Council), who did not criticize Churchill outright—though he was critical of Churchill's "method of government," as he wrote in his diary and in a letter to his sister.

In many of the diaries and letters of those days, "unscrupulous," "unreliable," "ambitious," and "lacking political judgment" are epithets and descriptions applied to Churchill; "crooks," "wild men," and "gangsters" to some of his supporters and to his appointments. Remarkable,

---

*One person whom Churchill instantly told to leave was Sir Horace Wilson, Chamberlain's gatekeeper and grey eminence, a glabrous and sinuous appeaser. The full Cabinet had many members, at times more than twenty-five; the War Cabinet had only five (Churchill, Chamberlain, Halifax, and the two Labour men, Attlee and Greenwood, without much experience and of a minority).

and perhaps ominous, were the inclinations of many who thought that Churchill's government would not, because it could not, last. Jock Colville wrote in his diary on 11 May: "there seems to be some inclination in Whitehall to believe that Winston will be a complete failure and that Neville will return." On the same day Lord Davidson wrote to former Prime Minister Stanley Baldwin: "The Tories don't trust Winston. . . . After the next clash of war is over it may well be that a sounder Government may emerge."

Alex Cadogan, the principal adviser to Halifax, wrote in his diary that day that he could not think of a prime minister better than Chamberlain: "I'm afraid that Winston will build up a 'Garden City'* at No. 10, with the most awful people." R. A. (Rab) Butler, an archconservative, hated and despised Churchill. On the 12th he wrote that Churchill was "a disaster." C. M. Headlam, a stalwart, average Conservative member of Parliament and a Chamberlainite, wrote on the 10th about Churchill: "so at last that man has gained his ambition: I never thought he would—well—let us hope that he makes good. I have never believed in him: I only hope that my judgment of the man will be proved wrong. He certainly possesses courage, imagination, and

---

*A cheap modern suburb.

drive. . . . and age and experience and responsibility may give him judgment—than all should be well." But the next day, reading about Churchill's first appointments: "To me it is not an impressive combination and it will not propitiate the more angry of the Conservatives . . . "

The expectation among many Tories that the Churchill government would not last was wishful thinking, but it existed. There was a distrust of Churchill among the military too. Lieutenant-General Henry Pownall (who later in the war became one of Churchill's closest military collaborators) wrote even before the 10th of May that "great as are [Churchill's] uses is also a danger, never counting his resources to see if the objective is attainable. And he is *unlucky*. He was throughout the last war . . . a bad and dangerous failing." Some officers in the navy, too, distrusted Churchill. Hankey wrote to Sam Hoare, a principal opponent of Churchill through many years:* "God help the country . . . which commits its existence to the hands of a dictator whose past achievements, even though inspired by a certain amount of imagination, have never achieved success! . . . An untried and wholly inexperi-

---

*Soon Churchill made Hoare (Lord Templewood) British ambassador to Spain, where he performed his duties very well.

enced politician. . . . The only hope lies in the solid core of Churchill, Chamberlain, and Halifax, but whether the wise old elephants will be able to hold the Rogue Elephant, I doubt."

Then came the 13th of May.

AT 5 IN THE MORNING in Buckingham Palace, the telephone rang. The Queen of Holland was desperate; she wished to talk to the King. Her country was crumbling fast; her cities were bombed; she must leave for England. She begged for British planes. The King tried to calm her. Churchill knew that Holland was falling.* By noon the Queen was in London.

Churchill spoke to his cabinet ministers that morning. He had been preparing his speech in the House of Commons, his first speech as prime minister. He had tried out a

---

*Churchill also thought of another royal personage: William II, the former German emperor, living in exile in Holland. He sent a message to William, offering him refuge in England. William rejected the offer. The next day German soldiers would be saluting

key sentence on them. He said that he would offer "nothing but blood, toil, tears, and sweat." In the early afternoon he walked into Parliament Building. His appearance—wearing a dark jacket, dark-striped trousers, a gold chain across his vest, and a dotted bow tie, and carrying his high-crowned odd black hat—was somewhat old-fashioned, perhaps neo-Edwardian, portly and solid.

The post-Victorian, gaunt, high-collared Chamberlain had entered the chamber a few minutes earlier, at which point occurred a perhaps surprising but also disturbing demonstration: The Conservative members rose up and shouted and cheered, waving their papers for two long minutes at least. It was a demonstration of their emotions, of their loyalty to the leader of their party, but also more than that: there was their element of remorse, their regret for having, by their abstentions, contributed to Chamberlain's resignation the week earlier. When Churchill came in a few minutes later, his entry was an anticlimax: They still wanted Chamberlain, not him; the cheers were short and not loud, most of them from the Labour benches.

---

him in his courtyard. A month later he would see Hitler in Paris, a city that he had himself been unable to conquer. He congratulated him (with a sentimental message that Hitler dismissed with contempt).

Here is what he said:

I beg to move,

That this House welcomes the formation of a Government representing the united and inflexible resolve of the nation to prosecute the war with Germany to a victorious conclusion.

On Friday evening last I received His Majesty's commission to form a new Administration. It is the evident wish and will of Parliament and the nation that this should be conceived on the broadest possible basis and that it should include all parties, both those who supported the late Government and also the parties of the Opposition. I have completed the most important part of this task. A War Cabinet has been formed of five Members, representing, with the Opposition Liberals, the unity of the nation. The three party Leaders have agreed to serve, either in the War Cabinet or in high executive office. The three Fighting Services have been filled. It was necessary that this should be done in one single day, on account of the extreme urgency and rigour of events. A number of other positions, key positions, were filled yesterday, and I am submitting a further list to His Majesty to-night. I hope to complete the appointment of the principal Ministers during to-morrow. The appointment of the other Ministers usually takes a little longer, but I trust that, when Parliament meets again, this part of my task will be completed, and that the administration will be complete in all respects.

I considered it in the public interest to suggest that the House should be summoned to meet today. Mr. Speaker agreed, and took the necessary steps, in accordance with the power conferred upon him by the Resolution of the House. At the end of the proceedings today, the Adjournment of the House will be proposed until Tuesday, 21st May, with, of course, provision for earlier meeting, if need be. The business to be considered during that week will be notified to Members at the earliest opportunity. I now invite the House, by the Motion which stands in my name, to record its approval of the steps taken and to declare its confidence in the new Government.

To form an Administration of this scale and complexity is a serious undertaking in itself, but it must be remembered that we are in the preliminary stage of one of the greatest battles in history, that we are in action at many other points in Norway and in Holland, that we have to be prepared in the Mediterranean, that the air battle is continuous and that many preparations, such as have been indicated by my hon. Friend below the Gangway, have to be made here at home. In this crisis I hope I may be pardoned if I do not address the House at any length today. I hope that any of my friends and colleagues, or former colleagues, who are affected by the political reconstruction, will make allowance, all allowance, for any lack of ceremony with which it has been necessary to act.

I would say to the House, as I said to those who have joined this Government: I have nothing to offer but blood, toil, tears, and sweat. We have before us an ordeal of the most grievous kind. We have before us many, many long months of struggle and of suffering. You ask, what is our policy? I can say: It is to wage war, by sea, land and air, with all our might and with all the strength that God can give us; to wage war against a monstrous tyranny, never surpassed in the dark, lamentable catalogue of human crime. That is our policy. You ask, what is our aim? I can answer in one word: It is victory, victory at all costs, victory in spite of all terror, victory, however long and hard the road may be; for without victory, there is no survival. Let that be realized; no survival for the British Empire, no survival for all that the British Empire has stood for, no survival for the urge and impulse of the ages, that mankind will move forward towards its goal. But I take up my task with buoyancy and hope. I feel that our cause will not be suffered to fail among men. At this time I feel entitled to claim the aid of all, and I say, come then, let us go forward together with our united strength.

This was one of Churchill's shortest speeches. When he was finished, the Labour and Liberal members cheered him. Also Lloyd George: "It was fortunate that Mr. Churchill should have been put in a position of supreme authority. All members of the House from the bottom of their hearts wish the new Prime Minister well."

From the bottom of their hearts? No. We can sense the—at times suppressed—resentment of some of the Conservatives from the record of their remarks after Churchill's speech. One, Spens: "If this war be won we must have a coalition of all the main bodies of pre-war opinion in this country." Sir L. Albery: "Many people in the House and a great number of people in the country strongly resented the manner in which the debate was conducted and the vote taken last week." (Hear, hear.) "When history comes to be written Mr. Chamberlain could rest assured that he would be given his due. (Hear, hear.) If Mr. Churchill—as they all hoped he would—carried this country forward to victory it would still be largely due to the

policy which had been followed by Mr. Chamberlain."
(Hear, hear.)

The vote confirming the new government was routine
and virtually unanimous,* but without a sense of enthusi-
asm.

CHURCHILL'S SPEECH was not broadcast to the nation.
The British Broadcasting Corporation summed it up in
their regular news bulletins, first at 6 P.M., then at 9. They
cited that key sentence: "I would say to the House as I said
to those who have joined the Government: I have nothing
to offer but blood and toil and tears and sweat." (A small
inaccuracy: Churchill's phrase included one "and"; the
BBC version three.)

Churchill wrote his own speeches. It is interesting that
in his own written and then typewritten text he put "I have
nothing to offer but blood, toil, tears, and sweat" between
quotation marks. Where did he get it from? Oddly, this was

---

*The one exception was the ultra-Left maverick Maxton
(Independent Labour).

a paraphrase of words famous once (and only in Italy), uttered by the Italian patriot Giuseppe Garibaldi.* When, on 30 June 1849, the government of the short-lived Roman Republic voted to capitulate as the French army was about to enter Rome, Garibaldi spoke to the decimated group of his armed followers: "I offer not pay, not lodging, no provisions. I offer hunger, forced marches, battles and death."†

Beside the choice of these words, there was something more profound and more important: the change of tone. The government's promises and the patriotism of the previous years were bland and repetitive and not particularly inspiring. At this instance Churchill wanted to impress upon people—the members of Parliament but also the British people—that immediately ahead of them loomed not the prospect of a Good War, of triumphs near or faraway, but the prospect of plight and suffering in the face of disasters, indeed of disasters around the corner, so to speak: ahead lay no promises but threat. No other British political figure spoke or would have spoken thus, not even

---

*At a very young age—when he was 23 or 24—Churchill had thought of writing a life of Garibaldi or of Napoleon.

†"Non offro nè paga, nè quartiere, nè provvigioni. Offro fame, sete, marce forzate, battaglie e morte."

in May 1940, because no one yet thought that way about the war in Europe.

Churchill's phrase was pregnant, too, with two other allied elements. One was this aristocrat's conviction not to ever underestimate the mass of the British people. As he said on other occasions during that year: They do not mind hearing bad news.* Better than many men and women of his class, he trusted (and, often in mysterious ways, understood) the common people of Britain: more than their intellectual capacity, their willingness to listen to his words.† The other element was his trust and belief that people would respond to a call of sacrifice. Few people saw that at the time. One of them was the singular and then quite unknown George Orwell; he had written in March 1940 in an obscure little publication: "Whereas Socialism, and even capitalism in a more grudging way, have said to people, 'I offer you a good time,' Hitler has said to them, 'I

---

*On one occasion in October 1940: "I always hesitate to say anything of an optimistic nature, because our people do not mind being told the worst."

†General De Gaulle in his *Memoirs:* Churchill "knows how to stir up the heavy dough of the English" ("remouer la lourde pâte anglaise").

offer you struggle, danger and death,' and as a result an entire nation flings itself at his feet." Do not just appeal to
people's materialism; do not underestimate them.

It is quite unlikely that Churchill read Orwell's article.
But Garibaldi's phrase must have rung in his ear (perhaps
something like the march from *Aida*). "I offer not pay, not
lodging, not provisions. I offer hunger, forced marches,
battles and death." "I have nothing to offer but blood, toil,
tears, and sweat." The words and the music differ; I think
that "blood, toil, tears, and sweat" in 1940 were more
telling.

On that particular day, at that particular moment: for in
the very hour when Churchill spoke in that chamber in
London, the Germans were scrambling across the Meuse
while before them an entire French army (the Ninth)
crumbled. It was the decisive military event in Germany's
conquest of the west of Europe and of France.

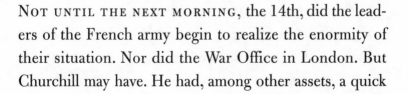

NOT UNTIL THE NEXT MORNING, the 14th, did the leaders of the French army begin to realize the enormity of
their situation. Nor did the War Office in London. But
Churchill may have. He had, among other assets, a quick

mind. Almost instantly, he recognized that this had become a new kind of war. Many years later he reminisced: "I did not comprehend the violence of the revolution effected since the last war by the incursion of a mass of fast-moving heavy armour. I knew about it, but it had not altered my inward convictions as it should have done." But now, for the first time, the thought that the French might be beaten out of this war must have flickered in his mind. We do not know. Certainly he would not have said so, even if he had felt it at the time.

On this 14th of May, the first day after Churchill's inaugural speech, the scene across the Channel was dark. In Holland the fighting was over; what was left of the Dutch army capitulated. The futile northward march of the French and British divisions had been turned around, and they were stumbling back across Belgium. The Royal Air Force sent bombers to destroy the bridges the Germans threw across the Meuse. Most of these brave but slow airplanes were destroyed, while the bridges were not. And something else was beginning to form, as well: a human tide of people fleeing before the German invasion. Automobiles and trains from places such as Antwerp were already encumbering the roads and rails of Flanders and France; soon behind them came people—sometimes entire villages and towns, horses and carts—crowding the highways and making the movements of soldiers ever more difficult.

The War Cabinet met twice that day. In the course of their secret deliberations emerged a consensus that the fighter planes of the Royal Air Force must be kept back in England. This agreement was not yet a decision: but it preceded by three days Churchill's and Air Marshal Dowding's historic decision *not* to send many more planes to France; to preserve the bulk of the Royal Air Force for a coming, perhaps approaching, battle of the air over Britain. Of course it was difficult to tell the French this. They and the Belgians (and, the day before, the queen of Holland) desperately thought and insisted that British airplanes should be thrown in to change the tide of the war. It was significant, too, that Churchill and the War Cabinet also decided against a bombing of the German industrial Ruhr, considering that the British strength in the air was not yet sufficient to respond to what they anticipated would be a severe retaliatory bombing of British industrial centers. In sum, there was an unspoken sense of agreement that the defence of Britain must be independent of what may or may not happen in France.

And the news from France was very bad. The War Cabinet still sat together when an urgent message came from Paul Reynaud, the French prime minister, telling

Churchill for the first time that the Germans were across the Meuse, with French divisions in front of them in retreat (indeed, melting away). Churchill went back to Admiralty House, retiring to bed a little earlier than usual, sipping his customary (and very weak) whiskey and soda, comforted by but one circumstance: that the reactions of the newspapers and of the British people to his speech the day before were positive, that "blood, toil, tears, and sweat" were the right words, the sounding of a bell with a deep, bourdon ring, a somber tone of warning.

He did not sleep very long. He was woken by an urgent telephone call from Reynaud at the unusual hour of 7. "We are beaten," Reynaud spoke with an agitated voice, in English. "We lost the battle."

Churchill tried to assuage and comfort him, and said that he would come over to Paris the next day.

THERE ARE A FEW HISTORIANS who wrote that Churchill's speeches and promises and prospects in May 1940 accorded neither with reality nor with his inner convictions; that his view of the world was like Dickens's Micawber's—hoping that something might turn up. Well,

Churchill's temperament was the very opposite of the cautious, slow, calculating, mouse-like Micawber; but that is not worth discussing. What matters is what Churchill knew Britain and Western civilisation were up against. It involved something more than the chances for winning if continuing to fight on. It involved his conviction, his deepest one, that if the Western democracies were to give up fighting, if they were to seek an accommodation with Hitler, that would be the end: the definite end not only of their independence but of Western civilisation, forever. On 31 May, in Paris, Churchill told Reynaud: "If Germany defeated either ally or both, she would give no mercy; we should be reduced to the state of vassals *forever*. It would be better far that the civilisation of Western Europe with all of its achievement should come to a tragic but splendid end than that the two great democracies should linger on, stripped of all that made life worth living."* In other words, fighting to the bitterest end would be more than a

---

*On 18 June, when France fell, he said in his speech (see page 108–111): If Hitler wins and we fail, "then the whole world, including the United States, and all that we have known and cared for, will sink into the abyss of a new dark age, made more sinister, and perhaps *more protracted,* by the lights of a perverted science." (My italics.)

grand gesture, it would be a potential asset inspiring future generations, something that centuries could recall and remember.

But then next to, rather than beneath, this faith *was* a calculation (or, searching for a better phrase, his view of the powers of the world at the moment). He saw that Britain had two choices: America or Germany.* Britain could keep its empire—a part of it at least—if she would accept the German domination of Europe. Or she could become an ally of the United States, its junior partner if necessary. To Churchill this was no choice at all—and not only because of his American connections. For Britain to accept one state and nation to rule all of Europe, including Western Europe across from England, would go against centuries of British tradition. And now that prospect was even

---

*He may have known that these potential alternatives had begun to form more than forty years before, sometime between 1898 and 1904. In 1899 Joseph Chamberlain (Neville's father) suggested in a speech a Teutonic alliance between Britain and Germany, to which suggestion the then Kaiser and his government were largely indifferent. Five years later an important element of Britain's *entente cordiale* with France was the British government's knowledge that Britain faced no threat from America; indeed, that the United States was now friendly with Britain.

worse, because Germany now represented and incarnated something even more ominous and dangerous: it was National Socialist and had become more powerful than ever. To choose Germany meant Britain would be not just a junior partner but a vassal state of Hitler's Germany, which was no choice at all, not even if and when France was to fall.

And thus, even during these days and nights of a cascade of dreadful news from France, the United States began to occupy Churchill's mind and time. Already late on the 13th, returning from Parliament, he asked the War Cabinet to agree that he would approach the United States, going directly to its president. On Thursday, the 15th, while preparing for his next morning's flight to Paris, he spent a fair amount of time writing a long letter to Roosevelt. The gist was this: "If necessary, we shall continue the war alone and we are not afraid of that." (That is: France may fall out, perhaps even sooner than later.) "But I trust you realize, Mr. President, that the voice and force of the United States may count for nothing if they are withheld too long. You may have a completely subjugated, Nazified Europe established with astonishing swiftness, *and the weight may be more than we can bear* [my italics]." "All I ask you now is that you should proclaim nonbelligerency, which would mean that you would help us with everything short of actually engaging armed forces. Immediate needs are. . . ." There followed a list.

Roosevelt's answer the next day was unsatisfactory, for more than one reason. He said that he could not commit himself to this or that without Congress. This was largely true. To this we may add the then very widespread isolationist sentiment of the American people, and the prospect of Roosevelt's unprecedented candidacy for a third time as president. There was another element: He was not yet inclined to respect and admire Churchill as he later would. He had maintained a confidential correspondence with Churchill since the very beginning of the war. The contents were kept as a secret between them, though the fact of the correspondence was known to Chamberlain and Halifax, who agreed to it. Roosevelt liked and supported Churchill's adamant recalcitrance against Hitler, but in May 1940 his assessment of Churchill was still uncertain. People around Roosevelt thought that Churchill was too old, too much of a Tory imperialist, and too fond of drink. Much of this assessment would change, but not yet. "I have nothing to offer but blood, toil, tears, and sweat" made no impression on Franklin Roosevelt. Unlike Churchill, he was not yet aware that France's resistance against Hitler's Germany might collapse—and soon.

CHAPTER THREE

CHURCHILL WROTE HIS LETTERS and speeches. That took some time. He went through his text, and changed and corrected words here and there.* Unlike Hitler, who wrote hardly anything, not even on the margins of important papers, Churchill was a man of the written word. We know that he had the eye of a painter, but he

---

*There are many evidences of this. A telling one is his speech on 22 June 1941, on the evening of the day that Hitler invaded Russia. He knew that this was coming; he thought long and hard

had (again unlike Hitler) just about no ear for music. Yet he had more than an ear for, indeed an often astonishing memory of, poetry. A consequence of that was his choice of memorable and often stunning words and phrases.

On occasion, Churchill rehearsed some parts of his speeches, speaking them out loud. (That he used the very words—"blood, toil, tears, and sweat" on the morning of 13 May before the assembled cabinet members is one example of this.)

There is a duality here. For a man of the written word, Churchill was very voluble—"grandiloquent," his critics would say. He would subject (and, on occasion, entertain) people around him with a torrent of words, phrases, remarks, ideas, often thinking out loud. Again unlike Hitler, who was very secretive, Churchill talked to people around him about whatever came to his mind. Sir Edward Bridges, the secretary of the War Cabinet, was struck by

---

what to say; he also knew that what he would say was directed to the people of not only Britain and Russia but also the world. He was busy that day, including a long lunch and a long dinner with many people; but he began writing his speech in the morning and made his last changes a minute or so before 9 p.m., when the technicians of the BBC were setting up their microphones in Chequers.

"the frankness and freedom with which [Churchill] would discuss things with us, or in our presence. When his mind was occupied with some important issue, he would often discuss it off and on for two or three days with those who happened to be summoned to his work-room. . . . In this sort of discussion he would keep nothing back. He would express the most outspoken views about the public reactions or attitudes of the most important persons, or about the various ways in which the situation might be expected to develop. And these confidences were not prefixed by 'You must not repeat this.'"* (Hitler, on the other hand, would occasionally remark to his secretaries: "Don't write that down.") His military advisers often complained about Churchill's loquacity; one of them joked that the prime minister had ten ideas every day, of which perhaps one was a good one.

Churchill's voice was not particularly impressive. He had a tiny lisp. More important was that he had to have a real audience. He almost always disliked talking into a microphone, to an unseen and intangible audience somewhere beyond him. It is not true, in most cases, that Churchill's speeches galvanized the British people the

---

*Bridges in *Action This Day: Working with Churchill* (London, 1969), cited in my *The Duel,* p. 112.

instant they were heard. Of course they mattered very much. But it was Churchill's vision that created his rhetoric, not the reverse. For a historian, the effect of many of his speeches is even stronger when they are read than when they are heard.

The impact of his great speeches in May and June 1940 was cumulative, not instant. The British Broadcasting Corporation's "Audience Research," a new practice, beginning only in May 1940, showed that 51 percent of the adult population of the United Kingdom listened to Churchill's first broadcast to the nation on 19 May, 59 percent on 18 June (his "Finest Hour" speech), and 65.4 percent on 14 July—a gradual increase. This rise amounted to something more than a conscious response to his words. It reflected an increase in the British people's trust in him and in his leadership.

But the "Blood, Toil, Tears, and Sweat" speech was not heard outside Parliament, except for the brief citation of the speech in the BBC news that evening. The words were read by some, not by many. Their echo and their impression appeared and grew, unconsciously, later.

In the week following his 13 May speech, only a few Conservatives were beginning to change their minds about Churchill. The diaries of the prototypical moderate Tory Headlam record his growing pessimism during the week after 13 May—but not pessimism about Churchill. On 19 May, after hearing Churchill's first broadcast to the nation, he praised it: "a fine, courageous effort—but there was no mistaking the supreme gravity of the situation." More revealing was the conversion of John Colville, a determined follower and former secretary of Chamberlain. On 10 May: "Nothing can stop [Churchill's] having his way because of his powers of blackmail." On the 13th of May: "Went down to the House to hear the new Prime Minister. . . . He made a brilliant little speech." Colville now went to work for Churchill. On 16 May he was still disrespectful: "his blasted rhetoric." But two days later: "Winston . . . is full of fight and thrives on crisis and adversity. . . . Such is the change that high office can work." Colville's turn had come: Soon he became one of the most loyal servants and greatest admirers of Churchill.

Two days after the 13th of May the gravity of the war situation was only just beginning to impress knowledgeable men and women, especially in London. Many of them were tight-lipped. The evidence of their pessimism appears only in a few of their reminiscences and their contemporary letters.

England had a free press in 1940. But its famous newspapers told the people little. Their reports of what was happening in Belgium and France were generalized, fragmentary, often unreasonably confident—in sum, often wrong. About this there was hardly any difference between the newspapers of the classes (e.g., the *Times*) and the masses (e.g., *Daily Mirror*), or between the Conservative and Liberal and Labour ones. The radio newscasts of the BBC were more succinct, but they, too, suggested not much of the stunning advance of the Germans. Much of this was due to a kind of self-censorship rather than official censorship, for the goal was to remain calm, to discourage pessimism, to not speak of panic. Even in the most serious newspapers, the news of the war—though not intentionally misleading—was entirely unrealistic. On 14 May, the headline in the *Times*—"RAF Triumph in Total War: 150 Enemy Machines Shot Down"—was entirely untrue, as was the dispatch: "French General Headquarters: 400 German Airplanes Destroyed in Few Days."

Oddly—or not so oddly—the newspapers tell us more now, more than sixty years later—not so much from their news items but from their other contents, including even their advertisements. They reflect a climate of the daily lives, and everyday interests, attentions, and sentiments of their actual and potential readership. Worth noting are the contents and choices of letters to the editor printed in the *Times,* the leading British newspaper, so often regarded (especially by foreign observers) as indicative of the inclinations of the British government.* On 11 May (the day after Churchill became prime minister), the *Times* printed a letter sharply criticizing Churchill's conduct of the Norwegian campaign. On the 12th there were two letters, one by a captain of the Royal Artillery (Scottish Command), dated 9 May: "Chamberlain [is] better qualified than most to head a determined people in its crusade. I welcome his leadership and pray for its continuance." Another such letter was written by the wife of a high navy officer. But by the 14th the editors chose to print a letter by a schoolteacher praising Churchill.† (Another letter, printed on 15 May,

---

*In May 1940 the editor of the *Times* was still Geoffrey Dawson, a definite and convinced Chamberlainite.

†"May we not at this crisis in our nation's fortunes take it as a happy augury that Mr. Winston Churchill is the first soldier to hold the office of Prime Minister since the Duke of Wellington, and the first officer of cavalry to hold this office since 'that terrible cornet of horse' William Pitt, Earl of Chatham."

merits inclusion here by virtue of its quintessential Englishness: "Sir. We are constantly told that the Germans are going to drop men by parachute in our back gardens, though I should not like to do anything of the kind myself. But do you not think, Sir, that people like myself who have shot, indifferently, it is true, in many parts of the world should be supplied by the Government with a rifle and ammunition? I don't say that I would hit the 'kamerad' as he was descending—that would be too much—but I would give a good account of him when he got into my potato bed. As things are I should have to go for him with a rolling-pin."

Reading the British newspapers of that time, one cannot but get the impression of an antiquated, more than old-fashioned, world. On the first page of the *Times*, where all notices and advertisements customarily were printed at the time, "Personnel Wanted" listings ran under these headings on 12 May:

Ladies' Maids and Maids
Cooks and Cook-Hands
Between-Maids and Persons
Kitchen and Scullery Maids
Married Couples and Manservants

On one of the main pages an article: "Entertaining in Wartime." "Luncheon Menus. A Simple Lunch." "Bean and Liver Casserole, Vegetable Curry, Macaroni and Rabbit Pie, Fried Carrots." (Not too appetizing but, then, English.) On the same page a poem by Horace in Latin, "Iustum et tenacem propositi virum;" and Kipling's "Lest We Forget." That week, the main cinemas in London were playing American films: *Gone with the Wind* and *The Postman Always Rings Twice.* (Just arrived.) Deanna Durbin in *It's a Date.* And even as Mussolini was making ready to declare war on England, the *Times* printed items about the then-famous music festival, the "Maggio Musicale" in Florence.

The newspapers were one thing. But we also have another, very valuable, source of the English people's thinking and of their morale. They are the typewritten summaries of Mass Observation.* The commercial research organization Mass Observation, or M. O., was created in England in 1937 (two years after George Gallup's Public Opinion Research Institute in the United States). Its original aim was commercial: to assist advertisers by

---

*Preserved to this day in the archives of the University of Sussex in Falmer, Brighton.

ascertaining popular likes and dislikes. By 1938, they were beginning to record people's attitudes about politics too. For us their records are invaluable because of their authenticity. They are reports of what was being said and heard, personally typewritten on simple pages (for the most part, by intelligent and serious volunteer women of the middle classes).

On 18 May 1940 the new Ministry of Information, led by Duff Cooper—one of Churchill's allies and friends—began to employ Mass Observation, requesting that they gather and submit their daily morale summaries to the government. Even before that date, Mass Observation had two long and significant reports on public and private morale. On 3 June, they had produced a very intelligent report, "Morale. Background Situations," covering the preceding months; another such summary was produced on the 14th of May.* The 3 June report begins with a critical summary of the unreasonable confidence with which most British people saw the war in the months after September 1939:

> . . . a feeling of confidence in our insuperable strength, an exaggerated belief in our armaments and defences,

---

*The first is File Report 125, the other File Report 105.

our own moral strength and Germany's moral weakness. The first seven months of the war did nothing to disturb this. And the belief grew [that] by waiting alone we should win, and that Germany was afraid to attack. Leadership encouraged the ordinary man and woman to believe that time was on our side, and in under ten months we were able to be ten times more confident of victory . . .

For not only were they overconfident, they were also underinformed about the actual facts of the situation. A barrage of success stories dulled the sense to all other aspects of the war problem . . .

[After the defeats in Norway,] when the real facts of the case began to come through, the people were staggered. Almost literally staggered. A terrific disgust and cynicism about all news sources arose within a few days, until nearly half of the population were openly and spontaneously complaining. . . . They felt the press and the BBC had let them down badly . . .

[Then, around 10 May,] not one person in a thousand could visualise anything like the Germans breaking through the Dutch water defences and into France. . . . [There is optimism, but that is] due to the inability of people to realise that we *can* conceivably lose in the long run . . . And a new feature is that many

69

people, while making confident or other remarks, use phrases and metaphors which imply a considerable uncertainty [in] or an admiration for Hitler's tremendous abilities. . . . [At the same time] there is no steady trend over the period, except the steady trend towards more and more doubt about leadership. . . . [lately] hundreds of over-heards, indirect and direct interviews and conversations, were collected every morning in London, Lancashire, and in East Suffolk villages.

There follows a statistical table, and its figures are telling. Optimism is the index figure 1, the relative proportion of pessimism either below or over that figure. Thus:

May 10–12 .82 (more optimism than pessimism)
May 13–14 1.45 (a great increase in pessimism, surpassed only—these figures were collected for every two-day period—on May 28–30, before the Dunkirk evacuation showed a definite prospect of success)

Now the Report of Mass Observation of 14 May, the day after Churchill's speech in the House:

The general unmistakable trend is a heavy increase in disquiet, particularly marked in London, in so far as our indications go. But the increase was not only quantitative, it was qualitative, to an even more marked degree, and for the first time a note that could almost be described as panicky was heard. . . . Similarly, optimism has declined from its 30% of the last three days to 19% today, and its quality has also declined. . . . Feelings of relief have now virtually disappeared, and recrimination has dwindled away to 2%. Uncertainty and bewilderment, and general 'don't know' is still forming a large group, now nearly a third.

Interest and anxiety were at their greatest in London. . . . As usual women are more anxious than men, and less optimistic than men, but the difference between the two has narrowed today, both sexes having reached their highest level for disquiet.

This suggests that Churchill's speech in Parliament, not widely heard, made no difference. The reason for the "disquiet" was probably the collapse of Holland.*

---

*And yet, on that bleak day of 14 May, an impressive event occurred. The new government called for men to register as Local Defence Volunteers at their neighborhood police stations. The

Mass Observation 125, composed three weeks after Churchill's speech, gave a summary of public opinion and sentiment during May:

> Despite a new leadership, it can by no means be
> said the mass of citizens are fully aware or awake to
> the necessities of the present or probabilities of the
> future. . . . We do not think that people are *essentially*
> or positively apathetic. They are merely negatively
> apathetic, because they do not know what they ought
> to do or how they ought to do it and under the new
> Churchill leadership they still fail in many respects. . . .
> There is a tendency among, for instance, people in
> the Ministry of Information to think that because the
> Government is changed . . . therefore, that the mass
> of people have changed too.

------

broadcast announcement was not yet over when thousands of men rushed forward; the police sergeants at their desks were running out of paper and ink; according to some reports within the next twenty-four hours nearly a quarter of a million men reported across the country—most of them middle-class men, to whom the government was unable to give arms, any arms, for long months yet. By the time they did, the Local Defence Volunteers had been renamed the Home Guard.

[And yet] The events of the last month [May], while they have upset and in one sense lowered morale, have actually improved morale in the strict sense of the word. For whereas before people were confident in victory, without a glimmering of what the struggle for victory might mean, now they realise to a considerable extent what they are up against. . . . But at least the period of utter wishful thinking is over.

"Wishful thinking is over." That was the essence, and perhaps the merit, of "blood, toil, tears, and sweat." A merit, rather than a result: we have now seen that an immediate effect it had not. Still, Churchill's heart now beat in accord with that of the mass of the people of Britain, though not yet with some of the representatives of his party, or with some of the upper classes or with some intellectuals. Never mind: the ending of wishful thinking had come. That meant much—but it guaranteed nothing.

CHAPTER FOUR

"THE BRITISH PULLED THROUGH." That was what most Americans thought in 1940, that is what they think about 1940 now, nearly seventy years later. England *held*, "*l'Angleterre tient*"—that was what most Europeans and the German-conquered people in Western Europe thought—but not until about September of that year. We live forward but we can only think backward. Or, in other terms: We judge events because of their consequences. Yet, while pursuing truths, historians must go through jungles of untruths. They know (or, rather, ought to know) that what happens is inseparable from what people think happens; but that inevitable condition was not necessarily thus in the past, when some things that happened were not always what people thought at that very time. In May 1940 the British people did not think—perhaps more precisely, they did not want to think, they did not allow themselves to think—that Hitler was winning the war. Perhaps he was winning his war against France but not against England.

But was he not? Few people in England saw that. Churchill did. England was not subdued—yet. But that potentiality had risen suddenly: it was there. "Blood, toil, tears, and sweat" were appropriate words. People had not recognized their full meaning yet; their reverberations would accumulate later.

Accumulating meanwhile were catastrophe after catastrophe. Churchill had a talent, at times amounting to genius, to see through things. But on the 13th of May, he (like all the other British military leaders) did not recognize the meaning of the rapid armoured advance of the Germans to and across the Meuse. Two days later, yes. After Reynaud's panic-ridden telephone call early on the 15th, Churchill decided to fly over to Paris, to find out more about the military situation, and to buck up the French. That was the first of his five hurried air trips to France during the next four weeks.

On the 16th of May, the sun shone relentlessly over Paris, as it did almost every day during May and June in 1940. But Churchill saw, too, black clouds of smoke rising on the left bank of the Seine, where French officials were burning the files of the Foreign Ministry in the courtyard of the Quai d'Orsay. The meeting was gloomy; the French commander-in-chief said just about nothing. Churchill was determined and vibrant and optimistic; he spoke and behaved thus to impress the French. (The clouds some of them remembered were those of his cigars.) It was more than a role he was playing. Churchill still believed—and that belief would persist for another week—that the advance of the German tanks was reckless, that a joint French-British counterattack, coordinated from north to south, could pinch off the snout of the German crocodile crawling westward.

But he knew something else, too: that the French leadership was tottering, that Hitler was winning, that he may be able to conquer all of France, and soon. He also knew, without saying so to the French in so many words, that he must not commit more British fighter planes to the war in France.

These two elements lived together in his mind. He thought of 1918 when, rather suddenly, the French and the British blunted the last great German offensive and turned the tide. He kept this hope even when, unlike in the First World War, the Germans reached the Channel ports Calais and Boulogne, and thus encircled the French and British armies to the north.

THE 19TH OF MAY WAS A SUNDAY. Churchill hoped to spend the day with his family in his house in Chartwell. This was not to be. After a War Cabinet meeting in the morning, his lunch was interrupted by a telephone call from General Gort, the commander of the British Expeditionary Force (BEF). The French armies were falling apart; a decision must be made whether or not to withdraw the British to the remaining Channel ports and thence to England. General Ironside, chief of the Imperial General Staff, did not yet think so; the counterattack of the British and French against the German spearhead was still possible. Churchill drove back to London for another meeting with his War Cabinet. Then he finished writing his first broadcast to the British people, which he delivered that night.

He said, among other things:

I speak to you for the first time as Prime Minister in a solemn hour for the life of our country, of our Empire, of our Allies, and, above all, of the cause of Freedom. A tremendous battle is raging in France and Flanders. The Germans, by a remarkable combination of air bombing and heavily armoured tanks, have broken through the French defences north of the Maginot Line, and strong columns of their armoured vehicles are ravaging the open country, which for the first day or two was without defenders. They have penetrated deeply and spread alarm and confusion in their track. Behind them are now appearing infantry in lorries, and behind them, again, the large masses are moving forward. The re-groupment of the French armies to make head against, and also to strike at, this intruding wedge has been proceeding for several days, largely assisted by the magnificent efforts of the Royal Air Force.

We must not allow ourselves to be intimidated by the presence of these armoured vehicles in unexpected places behind our lines. If they are behind our Front, the French are also at many points fighting actively behind theirs. Both sides are therefore in an extremely dangerous position. And if the French Army, and our

own Army, are well handled, as I believe they will be; if
the French retain that genius for recovery and counterattack for which they have so long been famous; and if
the British Army, whose dogged endurance and solid
fighting power of which there have been so many
examples in the past—then a sudden transformation
of the scene might spring into being.

It would be foolish, however, to disguise the gravity
of the hour . . . Our task is not only to win the battle
but to win the war. After this battle in France abates its
force, there will come the battle for our islands—for all
that Britain is and all that Britain means. *That* will be
the struggle. . . .

But there was an unfortunate element in this speech:
Churchill's stirring expression of faith in the French army.
"For myself, I have invincible confidence in the French
Army and its leaders. Only a very small part of that splen-
did army has yet been heavily engaged . . ." This counted
against him, especially among the Conservative members
who thought, and with good reasons, that Churchill's
Francophilia was leading him astray, as it often had before.
This unease and anxiety existed among many people of
the upper classes too, especially in London. Pessimism

and defeatism has come to exist also among intellectuals. At the same time, the tone and the substance of his first national broadcast made a good impression among the people, including a few political personages, while men and women of his staff had begun to see him as "indomitable."

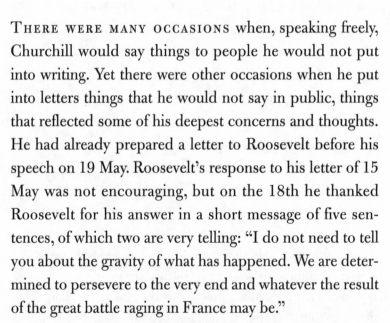

THERE WERE MANY OCCASIONS when, speaking freely, Churchill would say things to people he would not put into writing. Yet there were other occasions when he put into letters things that he would not say in public, things that reflected some of his deepest concerns and thoughts. He had already prepared a letter to Roosevelt before his speech on 19 May. Roosevelt's response to his letter of 15 May was not encouraging, but on the 18th he thanked Roosevelt for his answer in a short message of five sentences, of which two are very telling: "I do not need to tell you about the gravity of what has happened. We are determined to persevere to the very end and whatever the result of the great battle raging in France may be."

Two days later, on the 20th, he wrote his third dispatch to Roosevelt in five days. Again it was not a long dispatch*—but it included a startling, indeed ominous, passage: "Members of the present administration would likely go down during this process [the air war over Britain] should it result adversely, but in no conceivable circumstance will we consent to surrender. [But] if members of the present administration were finished and others came in to parley amid the ruins, you must not be blind to the fact that the sole bargaining counter with Germany would be the Fleet; and if this country was left by the United States to its fate no one would have the right to blame those then responsible if they made the best terms they could for the surviving inhabitants. . . . Excuse me, Mr. President, putting this nightmare bluntly. Evidently I could not answer for my successors who in utter despair or helplessness might well have to accommodate themselves to the German will. However, there is happily no need at present to dwell on such ideas." Churchill knew

---

*Thereafter many of his letters to Roosevelt would be long—and sometimes impractically so. Churchill had the usual writer's temptation to believe that a precise message, going from point to point, amounted to an important task accomplished. But dropping a letter in a mailbox, no matter how carefully written, is seldom the end of a story . . . especially not with the American president, whose attention-span was sometimes limited.

what few others knew at that time: Roosevelt thought that, if worse came to worst, the British fleet would leave and cross the Atlantic to arrive in Canadian and American ports.* A few (American) historians have suggested that these somber sentences of Churchill were meant to threaten the American president. They are wrong.

On Wednesday the 22nd, Churchill flew again to Paris.† By now the Germans had Boulogne and Calais surrounded. Late during the previous night, his staff saw him depressed; another somber wave of depression came upon him the night of the 25th. He did not know—how could

---

*The messages to and from Roosevelt were sent through the American embassy. It had to be that way—to avoid the resentment of Joseph Kennedy, the ambassador (the worst of Roosevelt's ambassadorial appointees), who was a defeatist and who trusted neither Churchill nor the ability of the British to withstand Germany.

†The day before, Churchill and the War Cabinet acted against their most dangerous potential domestic opponents. They ordered the arrest of Oswald Mosley, the leader of the British Fascist Party, and other extreme pro-Germans and Fascists. That day, too, they arrested Tyler Kent, a code clerk in the American embassy who secretly copied the Churchill-Roosevelt correspondence and gave the copies to foreign agents.

he?—what General Franz Halder, the chief of the German general staff, wrote in his diary on the night of the 21st, recording or summing up Hitler's remark that day: "We are seeking contact with England on the basis of a division of the world."

To the english people, "blood, toil, tears, and sweat" had not yet come. But Churchill knew that the entire war could be over and lost and soon. The fight must not be given up, because, if so, collapse and shame would stain their history forever. He peered beyond defeat. That is not the general impression of Churchill during the crisis, not even by his critics. His admirers, and even some of his critics, have recognized his courage. Hemingway once wrote that courage is "grace under pressure." That is a tawdry phrase. Courage is the capacity to overcome one's fear. But perhaps even that does not apply to Churchill. He feared not for himself; he feared for his country, for his people, for Western civilisation—large words, and yet the civilisation to which he belonged and what to him was all that he cherished. He and the British people must fight on—even if Hitler would win, that is, even beyond defeat.

This conviction Hitler did not understand. He underestimated Churchill. His mind fastened on what he knew or thought were the weaknesses of the man who was now—and, he thought, not for long—his principal adversary. He knew that Churchill drank. He knew that Churchill had money troubles. He knew that Churchill had Jewish friends who assisted him, at times financially. More important, he was convinced that Churchill's mind and character were hopelessly anchored in the past, regarding England and the world as they had been centuries before; he was a dissolute aristocrat, a reactionary. Hitler, throughout his career, despised reactionaries more than he despised Communists. They were hopeless, and they were weak.

There were elements of the British character and the Empire that Hitler respected and sometimes even admired. But in 1940, and for years before that, he thought that the British were old and tired, not made for a now present world. His meetings with all kinds of British Conservatives, including leading personages such as Chamberlain and Halifax, had strengthened that impression. They could, or would, or simply must agree to Germany's overlordship in Europe. He would not demand the dismantling of their Empire, much of which he could not inherit anyway. Their remaining ally in Europe, France, was on her way to collapsing now. This was the meaning of what General Halder wrote in his diary at night on 21 May: "We are seeking contact with England on the basis of a division of the world."

What these contacts were we do not know. (There were German attempts to contact France, via Swedish diplomats, arranged by Göring.) There were some attempts to contact British diplomats or others later, but it seems not around 21 May. (We must keep in mind that, unlike Churchill, Hitler was a very secretive man, and that throughout his life he used speech to impress others listening to him—in this case Halder.) But about one thing Hitler's instinct was largely right. Churchill's situation in London was not strong. He also believed that Churchill would have to go, sooner rather than later. About that he was, fortunately, wrong.

BUT DURING THESE LAST DEADLY days and nights in May, Churchill was suddenly face to face with two deadly dangers. One was the coming fall of France, and with it the fate of the encircled British army in western Belgium and Flanders. The other peril Churchill had to face occurred in the War Cabinet room at Ten Downing Street. The two perils were connected.

On 22 May Churchill flew to Paris again, where there was still some talk of a British and French attack against the German army around Arras. Returning to London, he already knew that this would not happen, and that a retreat of the British Expeditionary Force toward Dunkirk may have to begin. During the next three days Boulogne and Calais would fall—in spite of Churchill's at times impulsive and unreasonable orders to defend them to the last man. Late on the 24th, Friday, at the secret session of the top French government in Paris, the first voices of surrender were raised. Churchill did not know this, but he would not have been entirely surprised if he had.

But now there was another grave challenge in the closed room of the War Cabinet. Halifax, the foreign secretary, spoke up. He said that some effort to save England, to ascertain what the enemy wanted, should be attempted, probably through the intermediation of Italy. What Halifax said were not words of an appeaser or a sympathizer with Fascism or National Socialism. His was, perhaps, a voice of reason.*

---

*What now followed were those five days in London, 24 to 28 May, about which I wrote an entire book, *Five Days in London*. I must not recapitulate their history, but I cannot avoid summarizing their meaning.

Nine secret sessions of the small War Cabinet followed. The record of their discussions was not available to historians or other researchers until three or more decades later. And even that record is not complete (what historical records are?): In one session the secretary (Sir Edward Bridges) was kept out of the room during the first fifteen minutes, and there was a fifteen-minute talk between Churchill and Halifax in the garden on the 27th of which we can but surmise what they said—or, rather, what the first said to convince the second.

Halifax respected Churchill but he distrusted Churchill's ideas, his rhetoric, his impulsive temperament. Evidence of this exists not only in what Halifax said at the table of the War Cabinet but also in his diaries. He was reasonable, to which I add, also fair. On 26 May he met with the Italian ambassador, Giuseppe Bastianini, to whom he suggested that Italy—more accurately Mussolini—should know that under certain conditions the British government would consider certain discussions, so long as Britain's independence remained assured. Churchill thought that nothing would come of this in Rome, where Mussolini had decided to enter the war on Hitler's side. But Churchill also knew that once Hitler knew that the British wished to contact him, no matter how indirectly, the independence of Britain could *not* be assured; that with the slightest move in that direction Britain would have stepped "on a slippery slope" (another of Churchill's later memorable phrases). The public knowledge of any such attempts, no matter how limited, would crack British confidence and morale, not to speak of Britain's remaining ally and her remnant friends.

In those five days there were two fortunate elements beyond Churchill's eloquence. One was that nothing, or almost nothing, of the controversy between Churchill and Halifax leaked beyond the doors of the War Cabinet room.* The other element was that Chamberlain did not side with Halifax. Once or twice he showed himself to be in the middle, sitting uneasily on the fence, but he did not oppose Churchill. This was very important. Chamberlain was, after all, still the head of the Conservative Party, supported by the overwhelming majority of its members in Parliament. The two Labour members of the War Cabinet, Attlee and Greenwood, were on Churchill's side, but they were minority members, newcomers in the government, and not very knowledgeable of the military and international situation. Had Chamberlain sided with Halifax, it could not have remained secret for long. Yet that did not

---

*Surely not to the newspapers, whose articles and reporting continued to be insubstantial and even misleading.

happen because Chamberlain had changed his mind not only about Hitler but also about Churchill: He trusted, more than his words, his character.

On the last of those five days, 28 May, there was yet another clash between Halifax and Churchill in the War Cabinet. Many things were happening on that Tuesday. The evacuation of British troops from Dunkirk was beginning. Hitler was still waiting for something from London. In Tokyo, the Japanese foreign minister called the British ambassador and asked him whether he did not think that "Germany would soon make peace proposals."

The King of Belgium had surrendered the night before; Belgium was the main topic of the War Cabinet meeting at half past 11. The minister of information, Duff Cooper, talked of the need "for a frank statement of the *desperate situation* [my italics] of the BEF" at Dunkirk. He feared that unless that was given out, public confidence would be "badly shaken and the civil population would not be ready to accept the assurances of the Government of our ultimate victory." Churchill said that he would speak in the House of Commons that afternoon.

Then Churchill asked Chamberlain to talk with him privately. Their topic was not Belgium, not Dunkirk, but David Lloyd George. That remnant old champion of the

First World War against Germany had changed his mind about the Germans. In 1936 he had gone to see Hitler, and then spoke about him in most admiring terms. After the war had started, he spoke of the need to consider Hitler's peace proposals. Churchill and Chamberlain knew that. The trouble was that Lloyd George hated Chamberlain. Yet Churchill thought that Lloyd George ought to be asked to join the national government; and Chamberlain now agreed. (The letter inviting Lloyd George was sent the next day but the old man refused.) There can be no doubt that Churchill wanted him in to affirm national unity. But we may also surmise that there was another consideration in his mind: If the British army in Flanders were lost and Britain left shorn of arms, Lloyd George ought to be the man to deal with Hitler (and not some kind of British Fascist, such as Mosley).

Then, in the afternoon, Churchill went down to the House of Commons. He spoke briefly about the Belgian King's surrender ("I have no intention of suggesting to the House that we should attempt at this moment to pass judgment") and then about Dunkirk. He said that the battle there was going on; he would speak about it to the House in about a week (which was what he did). As so often, the meat of his speech came at the end:

Meanwhile the House should prepare itself for hard and heavy tidings.* I have only to add that nothing which may happen to this battle can in any way relieve us of our duty to defend the world cause† to which we have vowed ourselves; nor should it destroy our confidence in our power to make our way, as on former occasions in our history, through disaster and through grief to the ultimate defeat of our enemies.

At 4 o'clock Churchill returned to the War Cabinet room again. Their session lasted an hour. Most of it was taken up by Halifax and Churchill debating each other. Churchill went far enough to admit that the French might drop out of the war. Their desperate attempts at Italian mediation "were trying to get us on that slippery slope." Then he argued that Hitler's "terms would put us completely at his mercy. We should get no worse terms if we went on fighting, *even if we were beaten* [my italics] than were open to us now." Chamberlain, somewhat obliquely, supported Churchill. The Labour minority member Greenwood said that "the line of resistance was certainly a

---

*Another echo of "blood, toil, tears, and sweat."

†Note: more than only the cause of Britain.

gamble, but he did not feel that this was a time for ultimate capitulation." Halifax answered that "nothing in his suggestion could even be remotely described as ultimate capitulation."

Churchill adjourned the session at 5 o'clock. They would meet again two hours later. Within those two hours, he turned the tide. He had prepared for that. He had asked the so-called Outer Cabinet to meet in his room in the House of Commons, where he would speak to them. The Outer Cabinet consisted of about twenty-five persons of various constituencies, parties, and institutions, separate from the five members of the inner War Cabinet. Churchill spoke without a written text with but a small notepaper in his hand. Two or three versions of what he said exist. Churchill's version in his war memoirs, in "Their Finest Hour" volume of *The Second World War,* is the briefest. He omitted some of the things he said.

Churchill's version:

We were perhaps twenty-five round the table. I described the course of events, and I showed them plainly where we were, and all that was in the balance. Then I said quite casually, and not treating it as a point of special significance: "Of course, whatever happens at Dunkirk, we shall fight on."

There occurred a demonstration which, considering the character of the gathering—twenty-five experienced politicians and Parliament men, who represented all the different points of view, whether right or wrong, before the war—surprised me. Quite a number seemed to jump up from the table and came running to my chair, shouting and patting me on the back. There is no doubt that had I at this juncture faltered at all in leading the nation, I should have been hurled out of office. I was sure that every Minister was ready to be killed quite soon, and have all his family and possessions destroyed, rather than give in. In this they represented the House of Commons and almost all the people. It fell to me in these coming days and months to express their sentiments on suitable occasions. This I was able to do, because they were mine also. There was a white glow, overpowering, sublime, which ran through our island from end to end.

The fullest version is that by Hugh Dalton (who, erroneously, had feared that Chamberlain was the person ready to give up):

[Churchill] was determined to prepare public opinion for bad tidings, and it would of course be said, and with some truth, that what was now happening in Northern France would be the greatest British military defeat for many centuries. Churchill said: "I have thought carefully in these last days whether it was part of my duty to consider entering negotiations with That Man. It was idle to think that, if we tried to make peace now, we should get better terms from Germany than if we went on and fought it out. The Germans would demand our fleet—that would be called 'disarmament'—our naval bases, and much else. We should become a slave state, though a British government which would be Hitler's puppet would be set up—under Mosley or some such person. And where should we be at the end of all that? On the other side, we had immense reserves and advantages." Therefore, he said, "We shall go on and we shall fight it out, here or elsewhere, and if at last the long story is to end, it were better it should end, not through surrender, but only when we are rolling senseless on the ground." There was a murmur of approval round the table, in which I think Amery, Lord Lloyd, and I [Dalton] were loudest. Not much more was said. No one expressed even the faintest flicker of dissent.

Whatever Churchill said, he certainly did not say it "quite casually."

Thirty minutes later Churchill returned to the War Cabinet. He told them that the cabinet ministers "had not expressed alarm at the position in France" but had in fact expressed the greatest satisfaction when he had told them that there was no chance of giving up the struggle. Churchill "did not remember having ever heard a gathering of persons occupying high places in political life express themselves so emphatically."

Halifax now gave up. He only suggested that another appeal to Roosevelt be made. Churchill said no, that this would be premature.

CHAPTER FIVE

WHEN CHURCHILL NEXT spoke to Parliament, on 4 June, Dunkirk was over. He delivered one of his great speeches—for some, *the* greatest—the first whose phrases reverberated through England.

Was Dunkirk Churchill's deliverance? Many people, including historians, have thought so. It was, but also it was not. Had he not said that "whatever may happen at Dunkirk we will fight on?" *Whatever:* Keep in mind that on that day, 28 May, the evacuation from Dunkirk had only begun. Churchill himself thought that at best 50,000 of

the more than 220,000 British troops encircled in
Dunkirk could be saved and brought back to Britain. A
day or two later the prospects brightened, and in a week
almost 340,000, including 110,000 French, had been
saved. Through difficult and at times uninspiring—and at
other times very inspiring—efforts they were gathered,
corraled, sailed back to England. Some of these men truly
paid the price of nothing but "blood, toil, tears, and
sweat." (Tears, because many thousands had to be left behind as prisoners in Germany for almost five years.)

Churchill's speech of 4 June turned out to be one of his
most famous speeches. It was a long and full and often
brilliant reconstitution of what had happened at Dunkirk
and what it all meant; it was made to assuage and to raise
spirits, which it did. His rhetoric was not devoid of real-
ism. He said at the beginning: "We must be careful not to
assign [to] this deliverance the attributes of a victory. Wars
are not won by evacuations."* As so often, his most memorable words came at the end of his speech:

---

*A day later he saw General Montgomery, who complained bitterly
of how many people saw Dunkirk as a kind of victory. Montgomery
was not a major figure at that time. About him and Churchill, see
page 142.

Even though large tracts of Europe and many old and famous States have fallen or may fall into the grip of the Gestapo and all the odious apparatus of Nazi rule, we shall not flag or fail. We shall go on to the end. We shall fight in France, we shall fight on the seas and oceans, we shall fight with growing confidence and growing strength in the air, we shall defend our island, whatever the cost may be. We shall fight on the beaches, we shall fight on the landing grounds, we shall fight in the fields and in the streets, we shall fight in the hills; we shall never surrender, and even if, which I do not for a moment believe, this island or a large part of it were subjugated and starving, then our Empire beyond the seas, armed and guarded by the British Fleet, would carry on the struggle, until, in God's good time, the new world, with all its power and might, steps forth to the rescue and the liberation of the old.

The effect of this speech was great. Most of Churchill's opponents within the ranks of the Conservative members had already ceased to murmur or hum; this was the first time that some of them began to not only consent to but appreciate his leadership. Among the mass of the British people the approval was close to unanimous; he lifted their spirits. Of course so did the "deliverance" of

Dunkirk. Three weeks before, "blood, toil, tears, and sweat" rang with a thump of an unaccustomed music. Now there was another new sound, the sometimes Elizabethan ring of Churchill's phrases, with its recollection of Britain's history, a reminder of the presence of the past in their collective life. Much later, but not on or soon after the 4th of June, some British intellectuals (Kenneth Clark, Malcolm Muggeridge, and Evelyn Waugh among them) would say that they did not quite like Churchill's "Augustan" language. Other British writers and thinkers of very different stripes felt and on occasion wrote that their hearts and their courage were lifted by Churchill's unaccustomed and old-fashioned phrases.

AND NOW DISASTER FOLLOWED disaster again. Piecemeal but fast France was collapsing. Twice again Churchill flew to Paris. His purpose was to commit the French to keep up fighting *somewhere*; to keep the great new French fleet alive, somewhere beyond the reach of the Germans. But Churchill's flying trips were of no use. On 10 June, Mussolini's Italy declared war on France and Britain. Four days later Paris fell.

Churchill was now overworked, willing to take desperate steps, including a strange proposal of a union of France with Great Britain. On the night of 16 June, two days after Paris fell, he was about to board a train to speed him to yet another meeting, this one in Brittany with the French premier, when a breathless secretary ran up with the news that this was useless, the French war government was gone. Reynaud had given up to Pétain, the head of the party of surrender.

CHURCHILL SPOKE NEXT on 18 June—the 125th anniversary of the Battle of Waterloo, when Britain became the chief victor over a power that had dominated most of Europe. Now, 125 years later, another power had achieved that domination . . . and how!

By that morning, it was evident that the French had stopped fighting, that their new government would try to accommodate itself to Hitler. On that sun-laden day, Hitler was expecting Mussolini. They met in Munich. Mussolini and his son-in-law, Foreign Minister Galeazzo Ciano, were disappointed because the Germans had won the war against France alone; the Italian army had no results to show, no contributions to that triumph. Another disappointment was that both Hitler and his foreign minister, Ribbentrop, talked of peace. They wanted peace. They thought that the moment had finally come for England to give in. Hitler's spirits were high; there exists a photograph of him stepping out before his staff, laughing and slapping his thigh.

One signal had reached Hitler from Stockholm. A day earlier, R. A. Butler, undersecretary of state for foreign affairs (and thus second to Halifax), who had long distrusted and disliked Churchill, encountered the Swedish minister to London, Björn Prytz, in St. James Park. He asked Prytz to accompany him to the Foreign Office. There he told Prytz that "no opportunity would be neglected for concluding a compromise peace if offered on reasonable conditions . . . the so-called diehards [that is: Churchill] would not be allowed to stand in the way of negotiations." He asked Prytz to stay for a few minutes while he, Butler, went to see Halifax. When he came back, he told Prytz that Halifax had assured him that "common sense and not bravado would dictate the British government's policy"—though this should not mean peace at any price.

Hurrying back to his Legation, Prytz drafted an urgent telegram to Stockholm reporting on the conversation, and adding that in his view other prominent members of the Conservatives were tending to think that Halifax might soon replace Churchill as the head of the government. This news had an immediate effect in Stockholm, where the King, among others, hoped for a compromise peace between Germany and England. The Italian minister to Sweden telephoned to Rome that the British were about to discuss an end to the war.*

On June 18th, Churchill knew nothing of what Butler had done.† The day before, Churchill had decided that he must say something to his people about France. According to the BBC archives, about 52.1 percent of the population of Great Britain listened to Churchill's short statement. It lasted but two minutes, before the 9 p.m. news. His first sentence: "The news from France is very

---

*That was not so. The Italian minister thought that the British minister to Stockholm had an audience with the Swedish foreign minister about peace negotiations, which was not the case. To the Swedish foreign minister, the British minister said that the principle remained Churchill's "to continue the war with all our strength."

†More than a week later, Churchill asked Halifax about Butler. Halifax defended him, and the episode passed. Two years later Butler became an enthusiastic supporter of Churchill.

bad and I grieve for the gallant French people who have fallen into this terrible misfortune." His last: "We are sure that in the end all will come right."

THE NEXT AFTERNOON, 18 June, Churchill came to Parliament to make what would become his most famous speech. It was a long speech, lasting for more than half an hour. As so often, he rang the bell at its end:

> What General Weygand called "the Battle of France" is over. I expect that the Battle of Britain is about to begin. Upon this battle depends the survival of Christian civilisation. Upon it depends our own British life and the long continuity of our institutions and our Empire. The whole fury and might of the enemy must very soon be turned on us. Hitler knows that he will have to break us in this island or lose the war. If we can stand up to him, all Europe may be free, and the life of the world may move forward into broad, sunlit uplands; but if we fail, then the whole world, including the United States, and all that we have known and cared for, will sink into the abyss of a new dark age made more sinister, and

perhaps more protracted, by the lights of a perverted science.

Let us therefore brace ourselves to our duty and so bear ourselves that if the British Empire and its Commonwealth lasts for a thousand years men will still say, "This was their finest hour."

"Finest hour": These two words became (and remain) a famous phrase in the prose and speech of every English-speaking nation. But there are two other remarkable phrases within that same final paragraph.

"The abyss of a new dark age made more sinister, and perhaps more protracted, by the lights of a perverted science"—this is the first. Consider what Churchill was saying, and thinking: *A new dark age.* A few days before that, Reynaud, the French prime minister, had peered into the coming catastrophe: He spoke of "a new Middle Ages not illuminated by the mercy of Christ." But "a new dark age" was not "a new Middle Ages"; it was something much worse, *and perhaps more protracted.* If Hitler and his Germans were to win the war and subdue Britain, Churchill knew that this German domination would be more than the temporary success of an exalted demagogue: it could and would last very long. It would be more than the end of a war; it would be the end of an entire age of civilisation.

He profoundly understood the power, the vitality, the dynamism of Hitler's Germans. His contempt of Hitler was not allied with that usual and dangerous element of contempt which is underestimation. He also understood something that some historians even now do not understand: how advanced and modern German science and its achievements were—and could be. Hence "more protracted, *in the lights of a perverted science.*" The lights of a once-free Western Europe were now going out, extinguished by the Germans one by one. But another harsh light, a hard German torch, was capable of dazzling and blinding the sight of millions.

Another phrase in Churchill's concluding strophe, with its cadences, is no less remarkable. "Upon this battle depends the survival of Christian civilisation. Upon it depends our own British life and the long continuity of our institutions and our Empire." He understood that what Hitler embodied was more than the achievement of a dreadful historical episode of a tyranny, of a modern mass-supported dictatorship replacing liberalism, parliaments, democracy. He represented the end of a civilisation that had begun five hundred years before—and now the wave of a future overwhelming and drowning past and present. That was Churchill's historical vista. Within it there was no place for an isolated and weakened Britain, resigned to and bereft of an entire Europe ruled by one brutal, triumphant power. Churchill was Europe-minded. Halifax and Chamberlain and many of the British people were not.

But now there was yet another issue as well, that of the United States. "If we fail, then the whole world, *including the United States,* and all that we have known and cared for, will sink into the abyss. . . ." There were Americans in 1940 who did not understand this, some of them important and influential men such as Herbert Hoover, Joseph Kennedy, Charles Lindbergh—different men, with different inclinations and reasoning, not all of them entirely wrong. Roosevelt, for whatever reasons, would come to understand Churchill—but not yet. The desperate Reynaud had begged him to enter the war, but the President answered that he could not do so. On 15 June, Churchill wrote him again, urging Roosevelt to consider, seriously and startlingly, what might happen: "Although the present Government and I personally would never fail to send the Fleet across the Atlantic if resistance was beaten down here, a point may be reached in the struggle where the present Ministers no longer have control of affairs and when very easy terms could be obtained for the British Island by their becoming a vassal state of the Hitler Empire. . . . If we go down you may have a United States of Europe under Nazi command far more numerous, far stronger, far better armed than the New World." Among other matters, he asked urgently for American destroyers. But it took two and a half months before Roosevelt was able to commit destroyers to England. By the time they began to arrive in Britain another three months later, they were not of much use.

As on 13 may, the reception of Churchill's speech on 18 June was not unanimous but for a different reason. On 13 May there was a latent division in the House of Commons, where many Conservative members cheered Chamberlain rather than Churchill. On 18 June, Churchill's speech was greeted with near unanimity in the House but not among some people who listened to him as he broadcast the same speech on the radio later that evening. Headlam provides a fair sample of the average Conservative reaction to Churchill's speech in Parliament: "Winston made a very fine and courageous speech—I am not one of his admirers—[but] in many ways he is the right man for the present situation—his personality is what counts at the moment—and provided only that he does not run amuck as an amateur strategist, all may be well. At the moment he certainly commands the respect of the House of Commons and is very popular in the country. He looks very fat and unhealthy—but they tell me that he is in excellent form."

But on 18 June he wasn't. It was a difficult day, with an enormous agenda, involving all kinds of things—perhaps his most difficult day during the entire war. And in the end, to top it all, he was pressed—by some of his friends, including the minister of information—to repeat his speech to the people that night, on the BBC. Churchill rarely liked talking into a microphone, and on this evening his temper was particularly bad. It showed. Some people thought that he was drunk, or simply fatigued. "It was the poorest possible effort," wrote the newspaper owner Cecil King. Churchill's fervent supporter and admirer Harold Nicolson wrote in his diary: "How I wish Winston would not talk on the wireless unless he is feeling in good form. He hates the microphone, and when we bullied him, into speaking last night, he just sulked, read his House of Commons speech over again. Now, as delivered in the House of Commons, this speech was magnificent, especially the concluding sentence. But it sounded ghastly on the wireless. All the vigour he put into it seemed to evaporate." A report of the Ministry of Information next day said that "it was courageous and hopeful, giving bad news frankly, but there was some comment on its delivery."

Churchill was in a dark mood. He was irritable and abrupt and rude with some of his staff. His wife decided to warn him about his temper.

But speeches, like books, may have strange consequences. Soon none of the poor effect of that speech on the radio mattered. George Orwell made a percipient remark a few days later. "Uneducated people are often moved by a speech in solemn language that they don't understand word by word but feel to be impressive, e.g., Mrs. A. is impressed by Churchill's speeches, though not understanding them word by word." By October or November, his "Finest Hour" speech and also his earlier "Blood, Toil, Tears, and Sweat" speech began to circulate and reverberate, in print, and with effects well beyond the British Isles. People commenced to respond to them, nodding favorably, in Ireland, Canada, the Dominions, the United States—they were repeated, small jewels of the English language, on the threshold of entering dictionaries of quotations.

CHURCHILL WAS PLEASED with the effects of his spoken words; but, as he said a few days after 18 June (and repeated it in his war memoirs nine years later): "Rhetoric was no guarantee for survival."

Nor was it clouding his vision. One of his main concerns—the second most important one, after preparations against a German invasion—was to make something clear to Roosevelt, a hidden and awful business that could not be mentioned in public, certainly not in a speech. The essence of this was: No, Roosevelt, the Fleet will not go over to the United States. On 24 June Churchill wrote to the Canadian prime minister, Mackenzie King: "There is no question to make a bargain with the United States. . . . our despatch of the Fleet across the Atlantic should the Mother Country be defeated. . . . I shall myself never enter into any peace negotiations with Hitler, but obviously I cannot bind a future Government which, if we were deserted by the United States and beaten down here, might very easily be a kind of Quisling* affair ready to accept German overlordship and protection. It would be a help if you would impress this danger upon the President."

Two days later he cabled the same terms to Lord Lothian, the British ambassador to Washington, who had

---

*Vidkun Quisling was a public figure in Norway who accepted (and welcomed) the German invasion of that country and was ready to govern it thereafter under German tutelage.

suggested that Churchill make another speech. "No doubt I shall make some broadcast presently, but I don't think words count for much now. Too much attention should not be paid to eddies of United States opinion. Only [the] force of events can govern them." He repeated that if the Germans could invade and subdue Britain, "the British Fleet would be the solid contribution with which [a] Peace Government would buy terms. We know [the] President is our best friend, but it is no use trying to dance attendance upon Republican and Democratic Conventions."*

THE SURVIVAL OF BRITAIN was now the main matter. Her situation was grave. "Blood, toil, tears, and sweat" were no longer a warning, an exhortation, but an immediate prospect. Churchill was confident. He had to prepare

---

*At that very time, the Republican nominating convention met in Philadelphia in view of Roosevelt's projected third-term candidacy. Fortunately (for the British, who had nothing to do with that), it nominated not an isolationist but Wendell Willkie, an internationalist candidate.

his people, but he began to think that Hitler was not yet ready to try. His understanding of Hitler was a priceless asset. On 27 June he wrote to his friend General Smuts: "Obviously we have first to repulse any attack on Great Britain by invasion and show ourselves able to maintain our development of air power. This can only be settled by trial. [But] if Hitler fails to beat us here, he will probably recoil eastward. Indeed, he may do this even without trying invasion. . . ."

That was what came to happen; Churchill understood Hitler very well. But he did not underestimate the Germans. He knew that in late May or early June, German parachute troops could have descended on England, with incalculable consequences, even without strong German naval forces backing them up. Instead, after Dunkirk, Hitler's armies made for Paris, to the south. But now that campaign was done. England was alone.

"Finest hour," yes, but they were only words. They meant much for the British people. But for the rest of the world? And for Hitler? Hitler wanted to finish the war in the West. He hoped for a signal from London. If that would not come, he would order to prepare for the invasion of England. But he did not have his heart in that. Churchill sensed this. He had assured the British people;

he gave them hope and confidence. But he still could not offer them much more than "blood, toil, tears, and sweat"—much sweat.

CHURCHILL DEMONSTRATED his capacity to summon his people and their representatives not with a speech but with an act. That came on 3 July, two weeks after the fall of France and his "Finest Hour" speech. He decided to prevent the great French battleships from falling into German hands by destroying them, if he must. The result was the tragic sea battle of Oran (or Mers-el-Kebir).

France had a large and modern fleet, larger than that of Hitler's Germany, including several of the most modern battleships in the world.* Hitler's armistice terms to the French were, as the then British ambassador said, "diabolically clever." He did not demand the surrender of the still untouched French navy. He knew that if he did so, that powerful fleet would sail out of his reach, to Britain or the

---

*This was because of the French concern that, unlike in the First World War, they may have to fight Germany without the help of the British navy.

United States. His terms required the French warships to remain in French ports, not manned by Germans but under their supervision. The French admiral, Jean-François Darlan, decided to accept these terms; Churchill did not. To him these German conditions were very dangerous, perhaps even fatal. These splendid warships must not come into German hands.

Three of the fine battleships were in the French Algerian port of Oran. Churchill ordered the British admiral in the Mediterranean to approach his French counterpart and present an ultimatum: Set sail for Britain or cross the Atlantic to the Western Hemisphere; otherwise the assembling British warships would be constrained to sink them. Churchill admitted that this was "heartbreaking for me." But it had to be done. The French admiral, Gensoul, an honorable man, could not accept that ultimatum. The British began firing late in the afternoon of 3 July; they sank one of the French battleships, damaged another, and the third escaped. Twelve hundred and fifty French sailors died.

This strange battle, lasting ten minutes, had many repercussions. Important was the response in the House of Commons. When next morning Churchill reported to the House on the battle of Oran, the members rose enthusiastically and gave him a tremendous cheer. This now included all of the Conservative party members. Their indifference and their murmuring distrust of Churchill was now gone; they recognized how much Churchill had meant what he had said. All of his former questionable trust in the French and France was now evidently past. He was the champion of his nation, an English warrior.

Oran had a more than considerable effect elsewhere, too, especially in Italy and the United States. During previous years, Mussolini had thought and said that the British were no longer the descendants of their great empire builders, they were the last line of tired old men. Now Ciano, his son-in-law and foreign minister, wrote in his diary that what happened in Oran proved "that the fighting spirit of His British Majesty's fleet is quite alive, and still had the aggressive ruthlessness of the captains and pirates of the seventeenth century."

Another man, Goebbels, wrote in his diary that Churchill was a "madman." He and some others brought snippets of news for Hitler to the effect that Churchill's position was weak, that the Conservatives and others were divided. Hitler was interested in every fragment of such intelligence. But through July his mind was changing, gradually. On the 16th he gave his orders to prepare for the invasion of England. Three days later he made his long-awaited great victory speech in Berlin, offering peace to

England (or, more precisely, no continuation of the war with England) but nothing more. The speech had no effect in London. Churchill thought it best not to respond; he let Halifax do that a few days later. On 31 July Hitler, for the first time, ordered plans to be made for an invasion of Russia. Churchill did not know this, but surprised he would not have been.

CHAPTER SIX

DURING THE REST OF THE year 1940, its second half, Churchill still made a few remarkable and memorable speeches, most of them broadcast to the nation. On 14 July, France's national holiday, he directed his words to the French. They were noble words: "And I proclaim my faith that some of us will live to see a fourteenth of July, when a liberated France will once again rejoice in her greatness and glory." A principal element of his speech, broadcast to the British people, involved Europe. Britain was now fighting "*by* ourselves alone" but not "*for* ourselves alone."

London was now a "vast City of Refuge which embraces the title-deeds of human progress and is of deep consequence to Christian civilisation," the capital city of human freedom. By 11 September Churchill saw that the German air force was not winning the Battle of Britain. The bombing of London had already begun: Hitler had ordered that the battle be switched again from attacking the Royal Air Force and its airfields to attacking the capital. In a broadcast that night, Churchill rallied the nation:

> These cruel, wanton, indiscriminate bombings of
> London are, of course, a part of Hitler's invasion plans.
> He hopes, by killing large numbers of civilians, and
> women and children, that he will terrorize and cow the
> people of this mighty imperial city. . . Little does he
> know the spirit of the British nation, or the tough fibre
> of the Londoners, whose forebears played a leading
> part in the establishment of Parliamentary institutions
> and who have been bred to value freedom far above
> their lives. . . This wicked man, the repository and
> embodiment of many forms of soul-destroying
> hatreds . . . has lighted a fire which will burn with
> a steady and consuming flame until the last vestiges
> of Nazi tyranny have been *burnt* [his italics] out of
> Europe, and until the Old World—and the New—

can join hands to rebuild the temples of man's freedom and man's honour.

On 10 November Neville Chamberlain died. Late the next day a tired Churchill rose and began dictating his tribute to his once adversary (to be read not in the Parliament building but in Church House, where the Commons gathered during the Blitz). This speech was one of the finest creations of his prose, full of greatness and gravity, steeped thoroughly with his magnanimity.

At the Lychgate we all pass our own conduct and our own judgments under a searching review. It is not given to human beings, happily for them, for otherwise life would be intolerable. . . . In one phase men seem to have been right, in another they seem to have been wrong. Then again, a few years later, when the perspective of time has lengthened, all stands in a different setting. . . . History with its flickering lamp stumbles along the trail of the past, trying to reconstruct its scenes, to revive its echoes, and kindle with pale gleams the passion of former days. What is the worth of all this? The only guide to a man is his conscience; the only shield to his memory is the rectitude and sincerity of his actions.

Churchill read and reread the speech and gave it out to be read in advance of his delivery. He was pleased with it. He had reasons to be.

THIS ENDS MY CITATIONS from Churchill's great speeches in 1940. Still, for the rest of this book, I must return to its main theme, the first of them, the only one reprinted in this book in full: "blood, toil, tears, and sweat." For in July 1940 there were still five years of those yet to come.

The Second World War was "A Good War." This is an American expression that became current many decades after the war. Hitler had to be beaten, liquidated, eliminated from the world. The Japanese had to be beaten. All of these things happened. That it was not a good war to those who were defeated, and not for their victims during the war goes without saying, though it is worth thinking about. It was a good war because of the alliance of the British and the American peoples—and, most of all, because for every young American who lost his life in a two-ocean war, almost ten Germans and even twenty or more Russians died; few American civilians died; and the British, their soldiers and sailors and airmen and bombed and burned civilians together, lost fewer lives during six years than during the four years of the First World War.

It was a good war for Winston Churchill, too. By and large, he lived through it in high spirits, roseate with confidence, defeating illnesses and depression. Nearly seventy years later we are still inspired by his character. Nearly three later generations do not mind (to the contrary, they like) the pictures and the sounds of his inimitable presence, his grand words, his habits of good living, his drinking of untold bottles of good champagne and fine brandy and whisky and puffing his ever-present Havana cigars while great battles were going on. This was deserving of and befitting the man who was the sole obstacle to Hitler in 1940—not only because of his courage but because of his vision, of his view of history and the world. He thought—rightly—that Hitler and his new Germans were the greatest revolutionary force extant in the world, mightier and more dangerous than international Communism.

Churchill was the man who did not lose the Second World War. But he did not win it: Roosevelt and Stalin did. The victory cost Britain its Empire. Churchill knew that, and minded it, but he also knew that the imperial belief among the British people had been fading even before the war. If much of the Empire would turn over to the

United States, inevitably or not, as a price to pay for their alliance in defeating Hitler's Germany, for saving Britain from becoming, at worst, a vassal of the latter—well, then, so be it. This much we must understand, but we ought to comprehend something else too: That not only through that deadly dangerous spring and summer of 1940 but throughout the entire war, behind this horseman sat black care. As 1940 proceeded, and the "finest hour" came and went, Churchill gradually became ever more confident: He and Britain were not about to lose this war. But gradually he realized, too, that Hitler was not about to lose either—far from it.

In June 1940 Churchill thought and said: If Hitler does not win the war within the next three months he loses it. That was not so. Hitler did not win his air war against England; he adjourned the plan to invade England; but he was far from losing his war. Very far. Not winning a campaign did not mean losing a war.

Churchill, like Hitler, did not give much weight to calculations by economics—rightly so for the most part. But in 1939 and 1940 he knew of the nearly unanimous projections of official and unofficial economic experts that soon Germany would run out of essential materials of which Hitler's Third Reich had fewer stocks than had the Kaiser's Germany during the First World War. To win, Hitler had to win a quick war. There was some truth in this, but the economists' calculations were just about entirely wrong, at least for two reasons. One reason was the substantial supplies shipped to Germany from the Soviet Union during 1940 and 1941, when Stalin wished for Hitler's friendship. The other major reason was the astonishing efficiency of Germany's industry and economy throughout the entire war, providing both the war machine and the German people with their necessities better than during the First World War. By 1941, Churchill hoped that the strategic bombing of Germany might help force the Third Reich to its knees. It didn't.

But Churchill had reasons to be confident as 1940 went on. Roosevelt moved closer and closer to a virtual alliance with Britain. The Blitz, the German bombing, did not break morale in London. West of Egypt, British forces defeated an Italian army. Hitler's ally Mussolini attacked Greece and was pushed back into Albania ignominiously.

Yet this list of small British successes did not last. In

February 1941 a small corps of German troops was sent over to Africa led by the soon legendary Rommel; they beat the British and drove them back into Egypt. In March Churchill sent British troops to Greece; he helped to raise Serb resistance against Hitler in April but defeat after defeat followed. The German armies overran Yugoslavia and Greece in three weeks. Another British evacuation took place. Later in May a German parachute division wrested the island of Crete from a large British and Commonwealth presence there. It seemed that Hitler was on his way to emulate Alexander the Great in the Near and Middle East, perhaps driving to India.

Hitler drove against the Soviet Union instead. Churchill had expected that for some time. While Britain now had a new ally, Russia, that ally came to the verge of collapsing too in the fall of 1941. Early in September 1941, Stalin sent a memorable (though seldom noted) message to Churchill, asking for impossible measures of British help—including twenty-five British divisions to be shipped to Russia. The gist of Stalin's message was a sentence that was later omitted from a Soviet collection of documents: "The Soviet Union is in mortal peril."

THE AUTUMN OF 1941 in England was cold and dark. The German bombing of London had now diminished due to the mass moving of the Luftwaffe against Russia, but it did not cease. The prospect of victory, of an eventual end of the war, receded into darkness. Factories were cranking out machines, tanks, and airplanes, many but not enough shipped through black nights and ice to Russia. The circumstances of daily life, of shelter and food, were darkening too. Churchill had to face the awful prospect: If Russia was conquered by the Germans, what could he and Roosevelt do? The two had met off Newfoundland in August, but the president would not commit his country to declaring war on Germany. Hitler knew that. The day before his invasion of the Soviet Union, he gave a peremptory order to all German naval craft, including submarines, in the Atlantic: Under no circumstances fire at an American vessel, even if the latter attacks you, for that would provide the incident and pretext that Roosevelt and Churchill needed.

On the way back from their first summit, Churchill's battleship stopped in Iceland. There he spoke to British sailors. The war would last for another three years at least, he said. Not 1940, but this autumn of 1941 "was one of the bleakest times in British history," he wrote later. To Stalin he telegraphed later in September: "A long period of struggle and suffering lies before our peoples." Blood, toil, tears, and sweat: for Russia, now even more than for Britain.

Stalin, who was neither a great speaker nor a great writer, had nonetheless acquired the gifts of statesmanship. He recognized, as much as had Churchill, what the tremendous power of Hitler's Germany meant. What he said to Roosevelt's emissary Harry Hopkins at the end of July 1941 still holds the power to stun us nearly seventy years later: He said that Germany's might was such that Russia and Britain together may not be able to break it. What would change everything, he told Hopkins, would be an American declaration of war against Germany. Churchill thought the same. He said often in the autumn of 1941 that if he had to choose between a total American stoppage of arms and aid to Britain in exchange for a sudden American declaration of war on Germany, he would choose the latter without hesitation.

THEN WAR DID COME to America on 7 December 1941, but it did not change everything—at least not yet.

In Churchill's *History of the Second World War,* the reader can sense, perhaps even breathe, his great relief the moment the news of Pearl Harbor was brought to him on a Sunday evening (by his butler, who had just heard it on the radio). Then he instantly rang up Roosevelt. So we have won after all, he thought and said and nine years later wrote. Britain will live; the Empire will live. On a winter night, with darkness outside and inside, the news fanned the flame of his spirit. He (and Roosevelt) had known that the Japanese were about to attack. But where? And whom? Churchill had feared that a Japanese descent against *only* British possessions and bases in the Far East might not be sufficient for Roosevelt to ask Congress to declare war on Japan *and* on Germany. Averell Harriman, who dined with the Churchills at Chequers late in the evening of that 7th of December, recalled that Churchill was "tired and depressed." He spoke hardly at all. He sat glum, "with his head in his hands," for long minutes. Then the news came in.

Now Churchill thought, finally, that the war could not be lost. But did he think that the war—first, and foremost, the war against Hitler—was now won? The next morning he went down to Parliament and spoke. "It is of the highest importance that there should be no underrating of the gravity of the new dangers we have to meet, either here or in the United States." Two days later, he said that what the British must do is KBO, Keep Buggering On. Three words, less grave than "blood, toil, tears, and sweat" but essentially not different.

AND THEN, AS BEFORE in May 1940, came disaster after disaster. Unlike in May and June 1940, the disasters were unexpected. Was that Providence's sudden warning against a self-blinding optimism, against hubris? That we cannot know. What we do know is the list of disasters and what they meant for Churchill's vision of the war. He had ordered two of the greatest and finest British battleships to Singapore, to impress the Japanese. Three days after Pearl Harbor, Japanese torpedo planes sank the *Prince of Wales* and the *Repulse* within three hours. Two months after, Japanese troops marched into Singapore, where a British general walked out to meet them carrying the white flag for an abject surrender. Along the eastern shores of America, German submarines moved on their way to win the battle of the Atlantic. For six months the Japanese went from victory to victory. In a dejected hour Churchill said, privately, that British soldiers in this war did not seem to have the strength and the endurance of those in the war twenty-five years before.

Worse still: Hitler had mastered the fate that had befallen Napoleon 130 years before. His army could not break into Moscow, but it had survived the cruel Russian winter; now it was ready to march east and break the Russian armies again. Churchill understood full well what this meant. In February 1942, he spoke to the gallant Polish war leader, General Sikorski, in London. Sikorski implored Churchill to be tough with Stalin, for everything indicated that the Russians wanted to dominate Poland. Churchill replied that "his own assessment of Russia did not differ much" from Sikorski's. But he "underlined the reasons which made it necessary" to have a British agreement with Russia. "She was the only country that had fought against the Germans with success. She has destroyed millions of German soldiers, *and at present the aim of the war seemed not so much victory as the death or survival of our allied nations. Should Russia come to an agreement with the Reich* [italics mine], all would be lost. It must not happen." He went on: "If Russia was victorious, she would decide on her frontiers without consulting

Great Britain; should she lose the war, the agreement would lose all of its importance."*

In August 1942 Churchill flew halfway across the globe to talk with Stalin. Stalin's disappointment in—worse, his lack of understanding of—the necessarily limited and cautious and slow conduct of the British and American war against Germany was very dangerous. Churchill undertook this journey to tell him that there would be no Anglo-American landing in Western Europe in 1942. His personality and character had an effect on Stalin, but the danger of Russia ceasing to be an ally against the Germans persisted. Churchill was, however, able to tell Stalin the news that an American-British invasion of French North Africa was coming soon. It came in early November, only a week or so after the first British victory against a German army in the war, the battle of El Alamein, where General Montgomery had succeeded in breaking through the German lines, forcing a retreat. Three weeks later, Russian armies encircled the Sixth German Army struggling at Stalingrad.

November 1942 was a turning point of the Second World War, what Churchill eight years later labelled as

---

*Documents of Polish-Soviet Relations, vol. I, pp. 297–298, London, 1961.

"the Hinge of Fate." But the war, with its manifold struggles, was not over at all—far from it. That was the emphasis of Churchill's phrases in his speech to the British people after the victory of Alamein. "This is not the beginning of the end," he said with emphasis, "but the end of the beginning."

CHURCHILL WAS CONCERNED about Russia and Stalin. But while there exist all kinds of evidence of his concern— as well as of his anxieties about the American attitude toward the Soviet Union as the end of the war was coming near—he said nothing about them in his public speeches. To the contrary: his praises of Stalin throughout the war often sound pompous and exaggerated as we now read them, while his public appreciation of Roosevelt and of the American commanders is unexceptionable.

His reasons for omitting any public (and often even private) criticisms of Americans were simple: he knew that he and Britain were dependent on them. Well after the war, he omitted, deleted, and left unmentioned almost all of his criticism of, and his concerns and anxieties about, Roosevelt and the American military leaders during the last decisive year of the war, 1944–1945. As Churchill explained later in a letter to Eisenhower, who was about to ascend to the American presidency in 1952, he did this with the supreme standard of American-British friendship in mind. (Eisenhower failed to appreciate this favor. He treated Churchill with inexcusable disdain in 1952 and thereafter.)

The main cause of Churchill's anxieties and disagreements with Roosevelt during the last year of the war was not, as many think, the American propagation of the piecemeal dismantling of the British Empire, especially in Asia. The main cause was Russia—its ambitions and its heavy presence in so much of Europe after the war. Churchill saw the dangerous extent of Stalin's aims well before the Americans. He saw the looming conflict and potential tragedy of the postwar world.

Six years after the end of the war, he gave the sixth volume of his *History of the Second World War* the title "Triumph and Tragedy." The triumph over Hitler may not have had to lead to a tragedy, but it did lead to a division of Europe, to an iron curtain, and to the development of a cold war, with all of its terrors, between the Soviet Union and the West. No American president or general and no Russian president or general would call the outcome of the war in Europe a tragedy. Churchill did.

He did not speak in public about this until after the war. Could it have been avoided? Perhaps not. After all, there was a consistency in Churchill's vision of Europe and Russia during the entire war, from 1939 to 1945, even including its first twenty-two months, when Stalin was a partner, at times even an ally, of Hitler. Churchill thought Britain had only two alternatives: either all of Europe will be ruled by Germany or half of Europe will be ruled by Russia—and half of Europe was better than none. After all, the lost half of Europe would be its eastern half, far from Britain; also—and we have evidence of this from some of his private words in 1944 and 1945—Churchill sensed that Russian and Communist rule might not last there for long.

There are reasons and occasions to criticize Churchill's wartime words and his treatment of Stalin and the Soviet Union, but shortsightedness is not one among them.

CHURCHILL NEVER UNDERRATED the power of Hitler and the German armed forces. Rightly so. In 1945, unlike in 1918, they fought to the last hour, in some places even after Berlin had fallen and Hitler was dead. But there is a consideration that I must advance at the end of this book. Churchill wanted to spare British lives.

After November 1942, "the end of the beginning," Churchill could offer something more than blood, toil, tears, and sweat; now he could offer military and naval and airborne triumphs. Yet there still remained plenty of the former. We have reason to believe—even though there is little written or spoken evidence of it—that he may have suggested caution to Montgomery after 1942. He knew that Britain would emerge from the war torn, wounded, and bankrupt. But there must not be rivers of British bloodletting as there had been in the First World War. If and when possible, British lives must be spared.

In his papers and speeches and in his war memoirs, there was no mention of his reluctance—more precisely, of his anxieties and doubts—about the Anglo-American invasion in 1944 of Normandy, France, Western Europe. But memories of the dreadful trenches and wires and mud and rain of steel, the mass deaths of the First World War, lived strong in his mind. Even more was his understanding of the strength and the resolution of Hitler and the German armed forces. Rightly so.

In 1942 he fortunately was able to dissuade Roosevelt and Marshall from a plan to begin a landing in France later that year (and thus relieve somewhat the Russians in the

east). That premature invasion would have been a catastrophe. The first half of 1943 represented the zenith of his
influence with the American leadership: He was able to
persuade them to go on from North Africa to invade Sicily
and knock Italy out of the war. But by December 1943, at
Teheran, Churchill knew that he and Britain were third in
order and rank beside the two giants, America and Russia.
(Roosevelt himself rudely suggested this.)

Churchill agreed to D-Day coming in May or at the lat-
est in June of 1944; but Stalin sensed his reluctance and
taunted him about it. We know that throughout 1944 and
even early 1945, Churchill argued and pushed to expand
the Anglo-American presence in Italy, for their armies to
enter Austria and at least some of the Danube basin from
the south, but the idea was rejected by Roosevelt and his
military commanders. This is not the place to ponder
Churchill's motives, which included his inclination to pre-
cede and thus forestall the Russians advancing into
Central Europe, except to say that here, too, one of his
purposes was to spare an unimaginable slaughter of lives.
He feared that after establishing a foothold in western
France, the British and American troops would still face a
hard and formidable enemy, solidly entrenched across
France, to be broken only at an untold cost.

That did not happen, but it took almost a full year after

D-Day to wrestle Hitler's Germany to the ground. Meanwhile, a week after D-Day, German rockets began falling on London, continuing their bombardment for nine more months. Blood, toil, tears, and sweat were present still. Victory was coming into sight, but throughout these months Churchill's mood was often somber. He was full of anxiety because of the Russian presence in the middle of Europe, and because he was unable to persuade the Americans, not Roosevelt, not Eisenhower, and—for awhile—not President Truman either, to be concerned with the imminent division of Europe.

THROUGHOUT MUCH OF 1945, Churchill was tired and worn, at times uncaring. In late July 1945, the British people voted the Conservatives out of office. Triumph and tragedy indeed.

There followed the last ten years of his public life. He was still spurred to and capable of making great memorable speeches, among them his "Iron Curtain" speech in 1946, his 1948 speech in The Hague exhorting Western Europeans to move toward a union, his 1953 speech in the House of Commons advocating an attempt to correct the division of Europe with Stalin's successors in Moscow. None of these belong within the framework of this little book, save perhaps one sentence that he uttered during his last presence as prime minister* in the House in 1955: "Which way shall we turn to save our lives and the future of the world? It does not matter so much for old people; they are going soon anyway; but I find it poignant to look at youth and wonder what would lie before them if God wearied of mankind?"†

WE KNOW WINSTON CHURCHILL'S speeches from reading them, not from hearing them. His words inspire us as we read them, proof that they have stood the test of time.

---

*He was prime minister again 1951 to 1955, the Conservatives having narrowly won the national election in 1951.

†Yet he ended this speech with his customary call for confidence: "The day may dawn when fair play, love for one's fellow men, respect for justice and freedom, will enable tormented generations to march forth serene and triumphant from the hideous epoch in which we have to dwell. Meanwhile, never flinch, never weary, never despair."

(The opposite is true of Hitler's speeches.) This was already the case very soon after 1940: In 1941 a collection of his speeches from 1938 to 1940 were printed in a book. This publication was an instant success in Britain, the United States, and Canada. And in October 1940, a phonograph company (HMV) made a disk of four of his speeches—the ones he delivered on 19 May, 18 June, 14 July, and 11 September 1940. It is worth noting, however, that Churchill himself did not feature them prominently in his six volumes of *The Second World War*. He included all kinds of documents and letters that he had written during the war, but not too many excerpts from his speeches— even though, as we know, he had prepared and written them with considerable care.

Churchill's "Blood, Toil, Tears, and Sweat" speech was neither broadcast nor recorded, except in "Hansard," the printed document of the sessions of the House of Commons.* But "I have nothing to offer but blood, toil, tears,

---

*It does not figure in a recent large book diagnosing and analyzing Churchill through his six books of *The Second World War* and their composition thereafter, in David Reynolds's *In Command of History: Churchill Fighting and Writing the Second World War* (2004). In this volume of 646 large pages, Reynolds reconstitutes how Churchill spoke of and then wrote of the war, pointing out to

and sweat" was no empty phrase. They were the words of a man who did not lose the Second World War, the war against the greatest revolutionary and most dangerous national leader of the twentieth century, Adolf Hitler.

---

us the discrepancies between the two. But about the events of May 1940, Reynolds writes: "Churchill's public rhetoric is not an exact guide to his private policy in 1940. Whatever he said to raise public morale, his best hope at this time was a negotiated peace with some kind of German government. His worst fear, despite his innate confidence, was that he would not live to see it." This is worse than a mistaken attribution of motive. It is entirely wrong.

Acknowledgments

I am very grateful to Signora Dr. Luisa Azzolini (of Milan), to Steven Breedlove (of the La Salle University Library), to my friends Philip Bell and Geoffrey Best, to Erin O'Neill (Archives Researcher of the BBC Written Archives Centre), and to Karen Watson (of the Mass-Observation, Special Collections Archive of the University of Sussex Library) for their generous assistance and advice.

Basic Ideas

Every great idea—whether embodied in a speech, a mathematical equation, a song, or a work of art—has an origin, a birth, and a life of enduring influence. In each book in the Basic Ideas series, a leading authority offers a concise biography of a text that transformed its world, and ours.